SHRUBS
IN COLOUR

an Amateur Gardening encyclopaedia

SHRUBS IN COLOUR

by
A. G. L. HELLYER
M. B. E., V. M. H., F. L. S.

Illustrated from water-colour drawings by
CYNTHIA NEWSOME – TAYLOR
and from line drawings by
G. R. KINGBOURN

COLLINGRIDGE BOOKS
LONDON   NEW YORK   SYDNEY   TORONTO

Published for
Collingridge Books by
The Hamlyn Publishing Group Limited,
Hamlyn House, Feltham, Middlesex, England
Printed in Czechoslovakia by
Severografia, Liberec

First published in 1965
Third impression, 1971
© A. G. L. Hellyer, 1965

ISBN 0 600 44264 0

FOREWORD

I have always been so grateful for good illustrations in books about plants that I have a special sympathy towards fellow gardeners who tell me that they know the plants they like but cannot always remember their names. In consequence it has given me great pleasure to prepare *Shrubs in Colour* in which every genus mentioned is illustrated.

I have been fortunate in having the services of Cynthia Newsome-Taylor to paint the colour plates and George R. Kingbourn to make the sketches which indicate the habit and size of the shrubs. Both have worked from living material and this has meant much travelling for Mr Kingbourn and the collection of hundreds of specimens for Miss Newsome-Taylor. This would have been quite impossible without the kindly co-operation of a number of people, notably Messrs Jackman & Sons of Woking, and the Royal Horticultural Society at Wisley from whom the bulk of the specimens came. I am particularly grateful to Mr Arthur Tome, the foreman at Jackman's nurseries, and to Mr C. D. Brickell, the director of Wisley, both of whom sent me many of the specimens so that I could be sure of getting exactly what I required.

Others have helped too, notably Hillier & Sons of Winchester and Mr Charles Puddle, gardener to Lord Aberconway at Bodnant, North Wales, and to all I express my thanks. I hope they will feel that the result was worth the labour.

The motif of a spade on each page is to give an idea of scale, but this must not be interpreted too rigidly as shrubs grow more strongly on some soils than on others. Moreover, ultimate size can be influenced by position, treatment and, most of all, by pruning. Mr Kingbourn's sketches are intended to indicate averages and no more, but I believe they will assist in placing shrubs wisely in the garden.

A. G. L. HELLYER

THE PLATES

SHRUBS IN COLOUR

ABELIA These are not showy shrubs, for the flowers are small and either white or soft pink, but they flower freely, some for a long period in summer, others in autumn when shrubs in flower are scarce, and all have a good bushy habit and neat foliage, which in some kinds is evergreen. All have a wide tolerance of soils, but most are a little tender and therefore most suitable for southern or western gardens or sheltered places. They like sun.

The species most commonly grown are *Abelia floribunda*, 5 to 6 feet high and through, with the deepest coloured flowers of any abelia, almost a crimson, produced in June, more or less evergreen leaves, but distinctly tender; *A. schumannii*, perhaps the most generally useful, 5 to 6 feet high and through, with lilac-pink flowers from July to October; and *A. triflora*, one of the tallest, sometimes 12 or 15 feet high, with small, white, very fragrant flowers in early summer, and the hardiest abelia. One other fine kind often seen is *A. grandiflora*, a hybrid between two beautiful but rather scarce species, *A. chinensis* and *A. uniflora*. It has pale pink, slightly fragrant flowers produced from July to September, or even later, makes a neat 6-foot bush and in mild places is ever-green. It is hardier than either of its parents, but not as hardy as *A. triflora*. A feature of all these abelias is that the sepals, often reddish or purplish, persist for a long time after the flowers and are quite decorative.

As a rule no regular pruning is required, but all dead or damaged growth should be cut back to live, vigorous wood in April. Sometimes abelias are trained against walls, a position which generally suits *A. floribunda* and *A. schumannii*, and then it will be necessary to thin growth in April, retaining sufficient strong shoots to cover the space available and cutting the rest nearly to the base so that they make more strong young growths for training in the following years.

Propagation may be by seed sown in spring in slight warmth, but is more commonly by cuttings of firm young growth under mist or in a propagating frame in July. Cuttings should always be used for *A. grandiflora* as it will not come true from seed.

ABUTILON A good many kinds are too tender to be grown outdoors in Britain except as summer bedding plants, and none is completely hardy, but two abutilons will survive in the milder counties or planted in very sheltered places. They are very different in appearance. *Abutilon megapotamicum* has slender branches from which the crimson and yellow flowers hang like little lanterns throughout the summer. In the open it will make a sprawling bush about 3 feet high and 4 or 5 feet through, but against a wall its naturally arching branches can be trained up to a height of 5 or 6 feet. Rather hardier than this is *A. vitifolium* which makes a stiffly erect bush, 12 feet or more in height and 6 to 8 feet through, with soft grey-green maple-shaped leaves and widely opened pale lavender flowers, a little like a small single hollyhock.

Both these abutilons like well-drained soil and warm, sheltered, sunny positions. Pruning is confined to removing, each spring, all growth damaged in winter and, when grown against walls, removing sufficient of the older or weaker stems to leave room for the rest.

Both species grow readily and quickly from seed sown in a frame or green-house in early spring. Often *A. vitifolium* will perpetuate itself by self-sown seed, the seedlings springing up in abundance all round the parent plants. Abutilons can also be increased by cuttings of young growth taken in spring or early summer and rooted in a propagating frame, preferably with soil warm-ing.

ACER (Maple) Most acers are trees, but the beautiful forms of the Japanese maple, *Acer palmatum*, do not exceed 12 feet in height and as much or slightly more through, and from a garden standpoint may be regarded as shrubs. Basically the leaves of all these forms are maple-like, *i.e.*, they have five or seven deep angular lobes, but in some these lobes are further subdivided into numerous

Abelia grandiflora

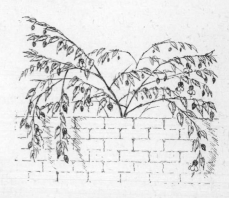

Abutilon megapotamicum

Acer palmatum

9

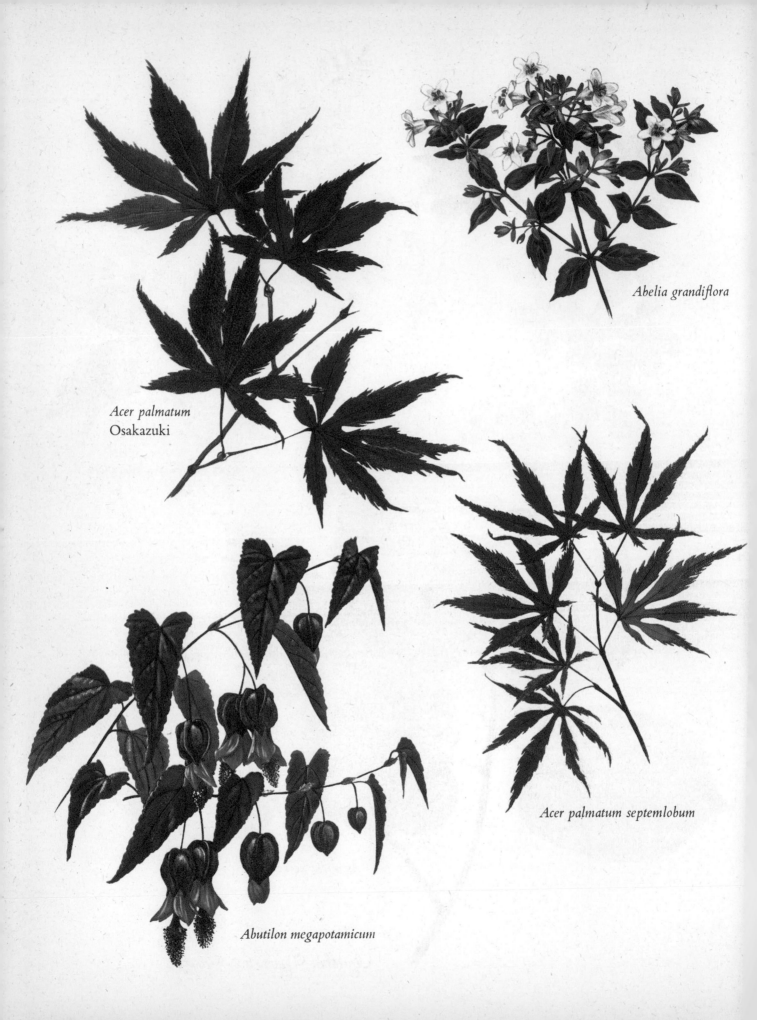

Abelia grandiflora

Acer palmatum
Osakazuki

Acer palmatum septemlobum

Abutilon megapotamicum

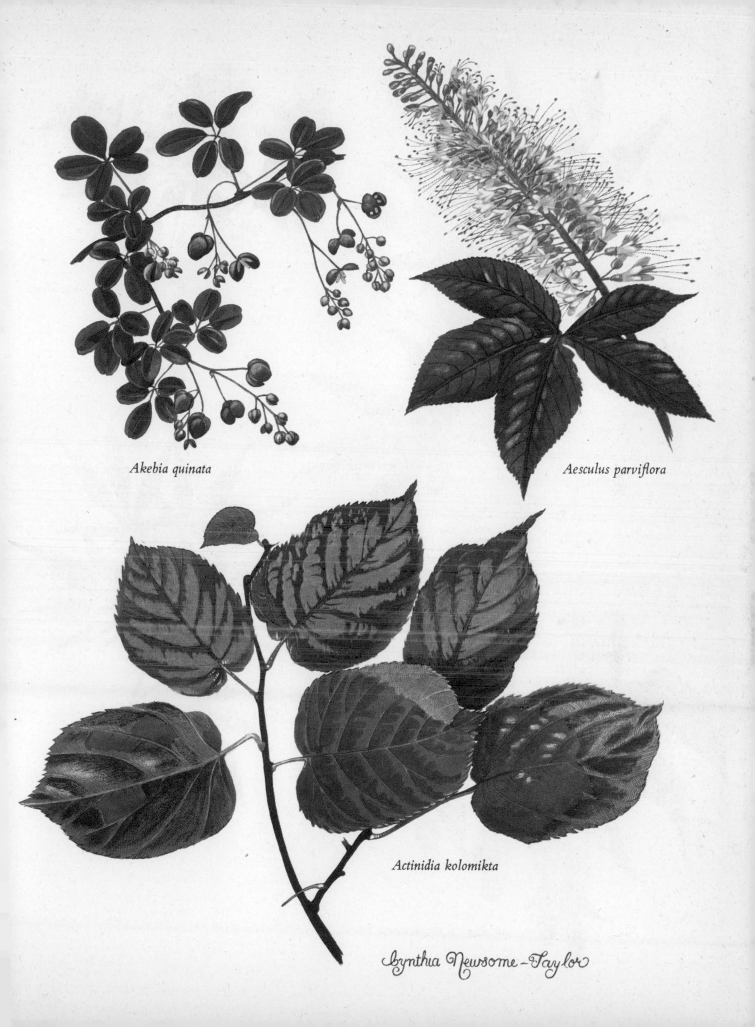

Akebia quinata

Aesculus parviflora

Actinidia kolomikta

Cynthia Newsome-Taylor

segment sometimes so narrow that they look more like the fronds of a fern than the leaves of a shrub. These leaf-divided forms have been given names such as *dissectum*, *filicifolium*, *linearilobum* and *septemlobum* which indicate their character. All colour in autumn, some more so than others, and some, such as *atropurpureum*, *dissectum atropurpureum*, *rubrum* and *sanguineum*, are purple or crimson throughout. One of the finest for autumn colour is Osakazuki.

All these Japanese maples thrive in sun or partial shade in a wide range of soils, but they dislike soil that is very wet in winter and in such places are best planted on raised sites. They require no regular pruning but if, as sometimes happens, branches are killed in winter or early spring by soil wetness or air frost the dead wood should be cut out at once.

Propagation of the choice garden forms is usually by grafting on to seedlings of *A. palmatum*, done in spring in a greenhouse. Seed saved from good forms of these Japanese maples will usually give quite good plants, but not necessarily closely resembling the parents. Seed can be sown in spring in a frame or greenhouse or in a sheltered seed bed outdoors.

Actinidia kolomikta

ACTINIDIA Climbers of which only two species are at all commonly seen in British gardens. These are *Actinidia chinensis* and *A. kolomikta* and the two are very different in appearance. *A. chinensis* is a very vigorous climber with big heart-shaped leaves and stems densely covered with red hairs. The flowers are white, changing with age to buff, and are followed by edible round fruits covered with red hairs, but it needs a good warm season to produce these. The plant is worth growing for its stems and leaves only. *Actinidia kolomikta* is much less vigorous, a plant to be trained up a sheltered wall where its leaves, many of them splashed with white and pink, make an unusual and decorative feature.

Both kinds thrive in good, loamy, reasonably well-drained soils. *A. chinensis* needs plenty of space and can be allowed to scramble through an old tree or over a large trellis or pergola. *A. kolomikta* is better on a wall. No pruning is required.

They can be raised from seed sown in a greenhouse, but the more usual method of increase is by summer cuttings in a propagating frame or under mist with some bottom heat.

AESCULUS (Buckeye) Most species of aesculus are trees but one, *Aesculus parviflora*, is a shrub 8 to 10 feet high and as much as 15 or 16 feet through, with candelabra clusters of white flowers, much like those of the Horse Chestnut, but not appearing until July and continuing into August. It enjoys a good, rich soil and a warm, sheltered position. It can be increased by seed sown in a greenhouse or frame in spring or by root cuttings in winter or early spring.

AKEBIA Two species of twining plants interesting for the small, fragrant, more or less chocolate-coloured flowers and large sausage-shaped pale violet fruits which, however, are only produced in warm summers. Akebias are worth growing for their abundant slender growth and elegant leaves, three-parted in *Akebia lobata*, five-parted in *A. quinata*.

Akebia quinata

They thrive in good loamy soils and sheltered but not sun-baked places. No pruning is required.

They can be raised from seed sown in a greenhouse, but the usual methods of increase are layering in summer or cuttings in July, preferably in a propagating frame or under mist with soil warming.

ANDROMEDA (Bog Rosemary) Small evergreen shrubs with little clusters of pink, hanging, urn-shaped flowers in May. Only one species, *Andromeda polifolia*, is at all commonly grown in gardens. In its typical form it is about a foot high and through but there are even more compact varieties such as *nana*, 9 inches, and *minima*, almost prostrate. The leaves of all are narrow like those of rosemary. All like moist peaty soils. They can be increased by layering in spring.

ARISTOLOCHIA (Birthwort; Dutchman's Pipe) Only a few species of aristolochia are sufficiently hardy to be grown outdoors in Britain, and the most popular of these is *Aristolochia durior* (also known as *A. sipho*), a vigorous twiner, called Dutchman's Pipe because the tubular flowers are curved rather like a pipe. They are certainly curious in shape and in their greenish-yellow and purple colour, but it is for its large, heart-shaped, light green leaves that this plant is primarily grown. *A. tomentosa* somewhat resembles it but has smaller leaves covered with down, most markedly on the undersides.

Both grow in a wide variety of soils and are quite hardy. They need no regular pruning and should be planted where they can ramble freely over trellis, old tree stumps or some other convenient support.

They can be increased by division of the roots in autumn or by cuttings in summer in a propagating frame or under mist.

Aristolochia durior

ARTEMISIA (Southernwood)   A good many artemisias are herbaceous or sub-shrubby plants, but *Artemisia abrotanum*, the Southernwood, is an evergreen shrub grown for its finely divided grey-green aromatic foliage. It will make a good rounded bush 3 to 4 feet high and as much through, but is all the better for being cut back fairly hard each spring, as this helps it to make strong young growth which develops its foliage to the fullest extent.

This is a shrub for light, well-drained soils and sunny places. Its enemy is winter wet. It is increased by summer cuttings in sandy soil in a frame.

ARUNDINARIA (Bamboo)   The naming of bamboos is so confused that I have included them all under this one genus as the most used and best recognised name in nurseries. There are many delightful species ranging from quite low-growing plants such as the 4-foot-high *Arundinaria auricoma* (this may appear as *Pleioblastus viridi-striatus*) to 20 feet high monsters such as *A. fastuosa*. Both these are fine garden foliage plants and so are *A. japonica* (*Pseudosasa japonica*), 10 to 12 feet high with dense masses of narrow leaves; *A. nitida* (*Sinarundinaria nitida*), similar in height, very graceful with purplish stems; and *A. murieliae* (*Sinarundinaria murieliae*) with rather larger leaves and yellow canes. All will thrive in a wide variety of soils, and though they look well by the waterside and usually grow freely there, they will also succeed in quite dry sandy soil. Cold winds, especially in spring, may cause browning of the leaves. All can be increased by division either in October or April, or rooted suckers can be dug up at these seasons.

Aucuba japonica

ATRIPLEX (Tree Purslane)   The chief value of the two species commonly grown in Britain, *Atriplex halimus* and *A. canescens*, is that they will stand a great deal of salt spray and so can be used as an outer protection for seaside gardens. Both are rather straggly in habit, though this can be improved by occasional pruning and trimming. Height and spread are 5 to 6 feet. Both are evergreen, but whereas the leaves of *A. halimus* are grey, those of *A. canescens* are nearly white. *A. halimus* is the more popular and generally useful shrub.

Both thrive in light, well-drained soils and sunny positions. They can be pruned any time in spring or summer as may be necessary to keep them in shape. They are increased by cuttings in summer in sandy soil, either outdoors or in a frame.

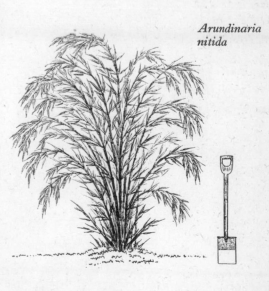

Arundinaria nitida

AUCUBA   Evergreen shrubs with large shining leaves, either light green or green heavily spotted and blotched with yellow. It is this variegated form that is most commonly grown and it is often popularly known as Spotted Laurel.

All are of one species, *Aucuba japonica*, a bushy shrub itself growing 8 or 9 feet high and as much through, but there are numerous garden varieties differing in height, habit and the colour of their leaves. The plants are unisexual, *i.e.*, some bushes will produced only male flowers, others only female flowers. The females can give fine crops of bright red berries in winter if there is a male bush nearby for pollination.

One merit of the aucuba is that it will grow in almost any soil and situation and does not object to dense shade. But to see its fine foliage qualities at their best it should be given reasonably good soil.

The common variegated form is known as *variegata*, and is female. Other

Andromeda polifolia

Artemisia abrotanum

Arundinaria japonica

Aristolochia durior

Arundinaria nitida

Azara microphylla

Aucuba japonica salicifolia

Atriplex halimus

Aucuba japonica variegata

Cynthia Newsome-Taylor

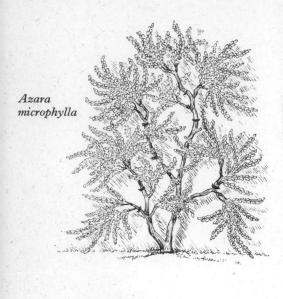

Azara microphylla

Berberis darwinii

Berberis gagnepainii

varieties are *crotonoides* with extra large leaves heavily variegated, available both as male and female; *hillieri* with very large green leaves and big crimson berries; *nana rotundifolia*, green leaved, very compact and 2 to 3 feet high, available both as male and female; *salicifolia*, a female form with long, narrow green leaves; and *viridis*, a male with bright green leaves.

No pruning is essential, but aucubas stand pruning well, so if it is desired to restrict them in size, or use them to form a hedge, they may be trimmed or cut back as desired in April or May.

The common form grows readily from seed sown in spring in a greenhouse or frame but seedlings may vary considerably so selected garden forms must be increased by cuttings; either cuttings of firm young growth taken in summer and rooted under mist or in a propagating frame, or fully ripe cuttings taken in autumn and rooted in an unheated frame.

AZARA These evergreen shrubs are all rather tender but *Azara microphylla* thrives well in sheltered places or against a wall and is well worth growing for its neat, shining green foliage and for the delicious perfume of its insignificant yellow flowers freely produced from February to April. *A. gilliesii* and *A. lanceolata* both have larger leaves and are more tender, but worth planting in the South and West.

If grown against a wall azaras will need an occasional tie to give support and to train the growth outwards. No regular pruning should be necessary, but misplaced or surplus growth can be removed in May. Azaras thrive in a wide range of soils.

All can be increased by summer cuttings of firm young growth in a propagating frame or under mist, preferably with soil warming.

BERBERIS (Barberry) This is one of the great shrub families with species, hybrids and garden varieties running into hundreds. From so great a number it is not easy to make a small yet representative selection. Those listed below are all good garden shrubs which have stood the test of time and they cover both the evergreen and the deciduous sections of the genus.

To take the evergreens first, the two most popular, and justly so, are *Berberis darwinii* and its hybrid *B. stenophylla*. Both are outstandingly beautiful spring-flowering shrubs. *B. darwinii* has little shining, holly-like leaves and short drooping clusters of orange flowers which may be followed by a crop of plum-purple berries. It grows 8 to 10 feet high and through and is densely branched. *B. stenophylla* is a little taller and broader and a good deal looser and more spreading, with narrow leaves and arching stems wreathed in deep yellow flowers which have a pleasant fragrance. It flowers a week or so later than *B. darwinii*, in late April and the first half of May rather than in mid-April and early May. It is also much easier to transplant. There are also dwarf varieties, 3 to 4 feet high and through, with garden names such as Crawley Gem, *gracilis* and *coccinea*, which are sometimes listed as varieties of *B. stenophylla* and sometimes placed separately under the name *B. irwinii*. There are also low-growing forms of *B. darwinii*, one named *nana*, another *prostrata*.

Similar in style to these but with even more richly coloured reddish-orange flowers is *B. linearifolia*. A fine hybrid has been made between this and *B. darwinii* and named *B. lologensis*. It has orange flowers. Both this and *B. linearifolia* are rather slow growing.

Berberis verruculosa is very compact, with shining spiny leaves and yellow flowers in late spring. It may eventually reach a height and spread of 4 or 5 feet but takes a long time doing it. *B. buxifolia* is usually planted in its dwarf variety *nana* which is 2 to 3 feet high but may be 5 or 6 feet in diameter. The deep yellow flowers are carried singly in early spring. Also low growing and even more spreading is *B. candidula*. The bright yellow flowers come in May.

Then there is a group of barberries with long, narrow leaves in tufts more widely spaced on the stems, so that they appear more open and less densely leafy. One of the best of these is *B. gagnepainii*, which will grow 6 or 7 feet high and 5 or 6 feet through and has yellow flowers in early summer, followed by blue-black berries. *B. hookeri* and *B. sargentiana* are stiffer in habit, with very long sharp spines and yellow flowers in spring.

The deciduous barberries are mainly grown for their berries but one species, *B. thunbergii*, is principally admired for the wonderful scarlet colouring of its foliage in autumn. It has a variety, *atropurpurea*, in which the leaves are deep purple throughout the summer. Both will eventually grow 6 or 7 feet high and slightly more in diameter.

Berberis aggregata and *B. wilsoniae* well represent the bushy, densely prickly type of deciduous barberry with yellow flowers in summer followed by heavy crops of coral-red berries. *B. aggregata* is the larger of the two, 7 or 8 feet high and through, against the 3 to 4-foot height and 6-foot spread of *B. wilsoniae*. Even more beautiful, because more graceful in habit, is *B. jamesiana*, a 10-foot bush with arching stems and long, hanging clusters of berries, at first pale green, gradually ripening through coral to crimson. *B. rubrostilla* is another free-fruiting kind with berries that are exceptionally large and long.

All these barberries are easily grown and have a wide tolerance of soils. They flower and fruit most freely in sunny places. No pruning is essential but, if desired, they can be reduced in size, in February or March for deciduous kinds, immediately after flowering for evergreens.

All the species will grow readily from seed which may be sown in early spring in a frame or in pots in an unheated greenhouse. Hybrids and selected garden varieties will not come true from seed and must be increased vegetatively. *B. stenophylla* produces suckers freely and these can be dug out with roots in autumn or winter and replanted elsewhere. Kinds that do not sucker can be increased by cuttings of firm young growth taken in July or August and rooted under mist or in a propagating box or frame.

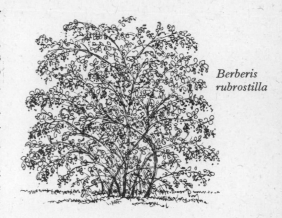

Berberis rubrostilla

BUDDLEIA Several very popular deciduous shrubs, one of which, *Buddleia davidii*, has become naturalised in some parts of Britain. This species flowers in late summer. The small mauve, lavender, purple or white flowers are sweetly scented and crowded into long tapering spikes or panicles at the ends of the branches. It grows very readily from seed, which is one reason why it has become naturalised. The seedlings show considerable variation in habit, size and flower colour and a number of the best of these have been selected and named. Royal Red is one of the most deeply coloured of these.

Buddleia fallowiana has much the same general habit but the leaves are silvery and the flowers pale lavender. Very different is *B. alternifolia* which carries its small lilac-purple flowers in May and June all along the slender arching branches.

The orange-yellow flowers of *B. globosa* are clustered together into little balls, also in May and June. A curious hybrid between this and *B. davidii* has similar ball-shaped flower clusters but they are a mixture of orange and purple. It is named *B. weyeriana*.

Buddleia colvilei is a more tender shrub suitable for sheltered places in the South and West. The rose-coloured flowers are much larger individually than those of the other buddleias, and appear in June.

All these are vigorous shrubs capable of attaining 10 feet or more in height and nearly as much in spread but amenable to pruning. *B. davidii* can be cut back hard every March if desired. *B. globosa* and *B. weyeriana* may be thinned and shortened in March but the pruning of *B. alternifolia* and *B. colvilei* is better left until they have flowered.

All can be increased by cuttings of firm young growth in a frame or under mist in summer or of riper wood in sandy soil outdoors in autumn. Seed can be sown in a frame or outdoors in spring.

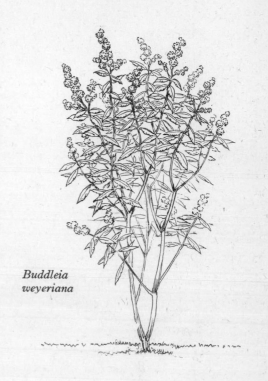

Buddleia weyeriana

BUPLEURUM Only one shrubby species is grown, *Bupleurum fruticosum*, an evergreen 5 feet or more high and through with blue-green leaves and clusters of small yellow flowers in late summer. It is mainly interesting because it will grow in very exposed places near the sea. It will also thrive on thin chalky soils but will grow equally well in other types of soil provided they are reasonably well drained.

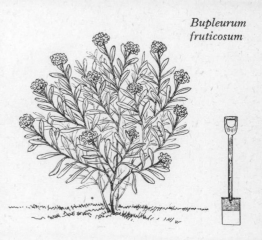

Bupleurum fruticosum

Berberis rubrostilla

Berberis darwinii in flower
and fruit

Berberis gagnepainii
in flower and fruit.

Autumn colour (far right)

Buddleia weyeriana

Buddleia alternifolia

Bupleurum fruticosum

Buddleia davidii
Royal Red

Cynthia Newsome-Taylor

Buxus sempervirens,
as a trained specimen

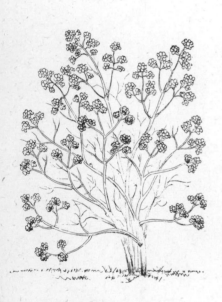

Callicarpa bodinieri giraldii
in winter

Calluna vulgaris

No regular pruning is required. Propagation is by cuttings of firm young growths in summer in a propagating frame or under mist, or cuttings of riper growth in early autumn in sandy soil in an unheated frame.

BUXUS (Box)   The common box, *Buxus sempervirens*, is a hardy evergreen most useful because of its dense habit and amenability to severe pruning. For this reason it is a favourite shrub for topiary and is also much used for hedge making. A special dwarf form of box, known as *suffruticosa*, is used for edging. There are also many other varieties of common box, some distinguished by leaf colour, such as *argentea* and *elegantissima*, both of which have a white edge to the leaf; *aurea-maculata*, which is splashed with pale yellow, and *aurea pendula* which has golden leaves and a weeping habit; and some by the shape of the leaves, such as *latifolia* with broad leaves and *myrtifolia* which has narrow leaves and a dwarf habit.

There are other species of box such as *B. harlandii*, a very compact, dwarf bush, about 3 feet high and through, with narrow leaves, and *B. microphylla*, similar in habit but with small rounded leaves.

All kinds of box have a wide tolerance of soil and situation. They will grow in sun or shade, on chalk, loam, peat or sand and are completely hardy. They can be increased very readily from summer or autumn cuttings in a frame, but the edging box is usually increased by division in autumn or spring.

CALLICARPA (Beauty Berry)   Deciduous shrubs grown primarily for the unusual colour of their small but abundant berry-like fruits. These, in the species cultivated in this country, are always in some shade of violet or lilac. There is some confusion in nomenclature as the species commonly grown as *Callicarpa giraldiana* should be *C. bodinieri giraldii*, and another good kind, correctly called *C. dichotoma*, may also appear as *C. purpurea* or *C. koreana*. A third species, *C. japonica*, masquerades as *C. mimurazakii* and *C. arnoldiana*.

All have a strong family resemblance and differ mainly in such details as size and breadth of leaf. The leaves of all take on pink or purple hues before they fall in autumn and all have a tendency to die back in winter, especially in cold places and on wet soils. Warm, sheltered places and well-drained soils suit them best. It is advisable to cut back each spring to sound wood. No other pruning is required.

Propagation can be by seeds, when available, sown in a greenhouse in spring, or by layers in autumn, or summer cuttings of firm young growth under mist in a propagation frame.

CALLUNA (Heather, Ling)   To the gardener there is little difference between *Calluna* and *Erica*. All, to him, are heathers requiring broadly similar treatment, having a general (but not quite universal) antipathy to lime and serving the same kind of decorative purpose in the garden. To the botanist *Calluna* and *Erica* are distinct genera and purists actually restrict the popular name 'heather' to *Calluna*, which has only one species, *Calluna vulgaris*. The many species of *Erica* are entitled only to the briefer name of 'heath'. It is, I fear, another case of the experts being out of touch with reality, for whatever they may say, popular usage (and that is the ultimate authority for popular names) applies heather indiscriminately to the lot and heather gardens are planted with *Erica* even more freely than they are with *Calluna*. Which is just as well, for the species and varieties of *Erica* cover a wide range of forms, heights and flowering seasons whereas all varieties of *Calluna* flower from July to October and the range in form and height is not great. The variety *foxii* is the shortest of them all, a nearly prostrate plant with very dark green foliage, and *cuprea* is in sharp contrast to this, its leaves golden in summer, bronze in autumn and its height, when doing well, around 3 feet. One of the most popular is H. E. Beale with double heather-pink flowers in long spikes and there are other double forms such as J. H. Hamilton, which is shorter and more spreading, and *alba flore pleno* which is white. The 'lucky' white heather with single flowers is simply known as *alba*.

All these forms of calluna, as well as the wild plant from which they have originated, thrive in acid soils. They love peat and detest lime. They also dislike being dried out in summer, a point often overlooked when making heather gardens on mounds and banks with no provision for watering in hot weather.

Pruning is not essential but the taller varieties can be kept more neat and compact by trimming with shears in early spring.

Propagation is by cuttings of firm young shoots inserted in sandy peat in a frame in summer or by layering in spring or early summer.

CALYCANTHUS (Allspice) There is nothing very showy about the two or three species of calycanthus cultivated in British gardens, but their maroon or reddish-chocolate flowers are curious and there is a pleasant aromatic fragrance about the wood and leaves, particularly strong in *Calycanthus occidentalis*, though *C. floridus* is probably a better garden plant, shorter and less straggling in habit and with warmer coloured flowers. *C. floridus* will reach 6 feet in height and spread, *C. occidentalis* 8 feet or more. Both are summer flowering.

They thrive best in deep, cool soils and do not like to be dried out while in growth. Ungainly shoots can be shortened in autumn. They can be increased by suckers removed with roots in autumn or winter or by layers pegged down at any time in spring or early summer.

Calycanthus floridus

CAMELLIA One species of camellia, *Camellia japonica*, has been a popular evergreen for a great many years and hundreds of varieties have been produced from it. Some of these have fully double flowers, some are semi-double, some single. The colour range is from white to crimson and the flowering season out-of-doors is spring, early spring in the South and West, mid to late spring in colder districts. At one time these shrubs were believed to be tender and were cultivated mainly in greenhouses and conservatories, but in fact they are quite hardy, though the flowers or flower buds may be damaged by frost. The leaves of *C. japonica* in all its forms are dark green and shining, making this a very handsome foliage shrub as well as a magnificent flowering one. Habit varies from spreading to erect, and very old bushes of some varieties may exceed 20 feet in height, but 6 to 8 feet high and through is more usual. If specimens do grow too large they can be cut back immediately after flowering.

Another species, *C. saluenensis*, has much smaller leaves and single soft pink flowers. It has been crossed with *C. japonica* to produce a race of hybrids known collectively as *C. williamsii*. There are an increasing number of named varieties of this hybrid ranging from single-flowered forms, very like *C. saluenensis* itself, to double-flowered forms very like *C. japonica*. Their particular merit is that they flower freely over a long period and that the fading flowers usually fall off naturally, especially in those forms which resemble *C. saluenensis*, so obviating the dead-heading (*i.e.*, removal by hand) of fading flowers which is necessary with most forms of *C. japonica* to prevent them looking shabby towards the end of the flowering season.

Camellia saluenensis

Two other species merit attention, *C. reticulata* which has a loose habit and produces very large single or semi-double rose flowers, and *C. sasanqua* which has smaller flowers rather like dog roses in the single forms, but there are also semi-double varieties. Both these species and their varieties are less hardy than *C. japonica*, *C. saluenensis* and *C. williamsii*, and should be given sheltered places against walls or in woodland, except in the mildest regions.

All camellias dislike lime and enjoy deep, cool soils well supplied with peat or leafmould, though they have a much wider soil tolerance than is commonly realised. It is often said that they like some shade, and they are certainly good plants for thin woodland, but the varieties of *C. japonica* will also thrive in full sun and usually flower most freely under such conditions, though growth is likely to be slower and foliage may be less green. Pruning is only required to keep plants in bounds.

Propagation is usually by summer cuttings and these cuttings may be of short lengths of firm young growth, or of individual leaves each cut with a small piece of stem containing a growth bud. These cuttings are rooted in sandy

Camellia williamsii Donation

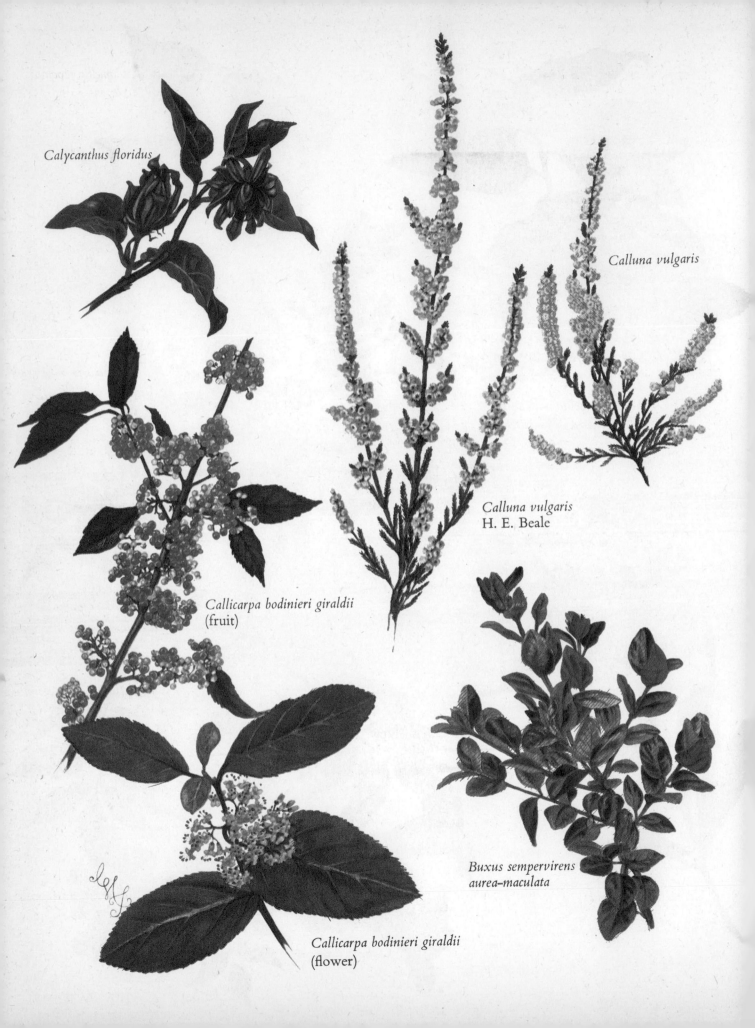

Calycanthus floridus

Calluna vulgaris

Calluna vulgaris
H. E. Beale

Callicarpa bodinieri giraldii
(fruit)

*Buxus sempervirens
aurea–maculata*

Callicarpa bodinieri giraldii
(flower)

Camellia japonica
elegans

Camellia williamsii
Mary Christian

Caragana arborescens

Carpenteria californica

Campsis radicans

Cynthia Newsome-Taylor

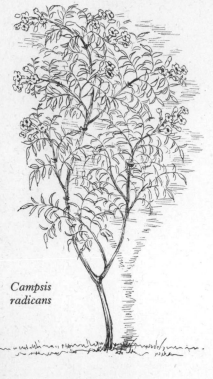

Campsis radicans

Carpenteria californica

Caryopteris clandonensis

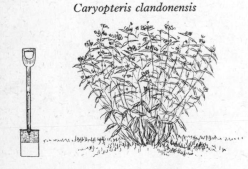

peat in a propagating frame or under mist. Branches may also be layered outdoors in spring or summer.

CAMPSIS (Trumpet Creeper) Vigorous climbers which will cling to walls, fences or other supports by means of small aerial roots like those of an ivy. The leaves are large and pinnate (*i.e.*, composed of numerous individual leaflets like those of an ash) and the flowers are large trumpets produced in late summer. These are very handsome plants and would be much more widely grown if they were hardier. In fact, all are subject to injury by frost, some more so than others, and all should be planted in warm, sunny, sheltered places.

One of the hardiest is *Campsis radicans* with red and orange flowers (or all yellow in the variety *flava*), but the blooms, though showy, are not so large as those of *C. grandiflora* which is also brighter in colour. There is a hybrid between these two species named *C. tagliabuana*, and a particularly fine form of this, known as Madame Galen, combines most of the good qualities of both parents.

The only pruning necessary is the removal of dead growth each spring, but if plants do encroach too far they can be cut back still more at this period. Propagation is by layering in spring and summer or by cuttings of firm young growth in summer in a propagating frame or under mist.

CARAGANA This genus belongs to the pea family and one kind, *Caragana arborescens*, is sometimes called the Pea Tree, though it is more a large shrub than a genuine tree. All kinds are alike in being deciduous and in having leaves composed of numerous small leaflets and those commonly grown in British gardens have yellow flowers. *C. arborescens* is the most familiar, a rather tall, narrow bush or small tree as much as 15 or 20 feet high, producing its flowers in May. It is by no means a showy plant but quite attractive and distinctive. There are several varieties of it including one, named *pendula*, in which the branches hang down instead of standing erect and another, named *lorbergii*, in which the leaflets are so narrow that the appearance is positively feathery. *C. pygmaea* is not quite so dwarf as its name might suggest, for though its slender shoots are pendulous they build up to a bush 3 or 4 feet high and through. The flowers appear in June.

All caraganas like sunny places and well-drained soils. They do not require pruning, but if they get too big, they can be reduced in size by some shortening of growth in early summer as soon as the flowers fade. They can be raised from seed sown in greenhouse or frame in spring or from cuttings of firm young growth inserted in a propagating frame or under mist in summer.

CARPENTERIA There is only one species, *Carpenteria californica*, a beautiful evergreen shrub from the southern part of California and Mexico. This means that it is none too hardy, but it will thrive in the South and West of Britain and in sheltered places or against sunny walls elsewhere. It grows 6 feet high and through, has long rather narrow leaves, grey-green beneath and large, white, fragrant flowers freely produced just after midsummer. This is not a fussy shrub so far as soil is concerned but it is rather fastidious about climate. W. J. Bean records that it failed at Kew, apparently because of fog, but succeeded in Cambridge, where the atmosphere was much clearer. Certainly it is a sun lover and a plant that likes well-drained soils, but it does not mind the damp air of Cornwall and Devon, where it succeeds well. No pruning is required.

Propagation is by seeds, by cuttings of firm young growths in a propagating frame or under mist in summer, or by suckers dug up with roots in autumn or early spring.

CARYOPTERIS (Blue Spiraea) There are two species, *Caryopteris mastacanthus* and *C. mongholica*, both similar in appearance and useful because of their late flowering. They are deciduous and have numerous rather thin greyish stems and small grey-green leaves. The flowers are small, lavender-blue, carried in little clusters in August and September when the effect suggests a rather tall, very shrubby Catmint. The two species have produced a hybrid, named *C. clandonensis*, the best forms of which are superior to either of its parents. One, named Kew Blue, has deeper violet flowers and there are others similar.

All kinds of caryopteris thrive in sunny places and well-drained soils but are not otherwise at all fussy. Except in very mild places, some growth gets cut back each winter and it is a good plan to assist this natural pruning by cutting back all growth to within a few inches of ground level in late March or early April, when the bushes will be more compact, not above 3 feet in height in place of their normal 4 to 5 feet, and with a better flower display.

Cuttings of firm young growths root readily in sandy soil in summer or early autumn and quickly make sizeable plants.

CEANOTHUS (Californian Lilac) These very beautiful shrubs come in the main from California and are none too hardy in Britain. However, hybrids have been raised and some of these are hardier than their wild parents and have the added advantage of a longer flowering season. There are both evergreen and deciduous kinds. Almost all have flowers in some shade of blue. The flowers are individually small but they are gathered together, sometimes in quite small thimble-like clusters, sometimes in larger and looser sprays.

One of the hardiest of the evergreen species is *Ceanothus thyrsiflorus*, a tall shrub which may reach 20 feet in time though it can be kept much less by pruning. The flowers are light blue and appear in June. *C. veitchianus* is very like it but is less vigorous and would probably never exceed 10 feet in height and spread under any circumstances. *C. dentatus* has smaller leaves and bright blue flowers, but the plant that often goes under this name in gardens is a masquerader which should really be known as *C. lobbianus*. As this is similar in many respects, it does not seem that gardeners need bother much about possible transposition of name. Both species are as vigorous as *C. thyrsiflorus*. Perhaps the hardiest of all the evergreen kinds is *C. impressus*, with small leaves tightly packed on the branches and neat clusters of deep blue flowers in May.

The evergreen hybrids are numerous and some are much alike. *C. burkwoodii* makes a good bush, 7 or 8 feet high and as much through, with bright blue flowers all the summer. Indigo is deep purple and continuous flowering from June to October. Delight is hardier than most but its flowering season is confined to May.

The deciduous varieties are all hybrids with garden names such as Gloire de Versailles, light blue, Topaz, a deeper blue and Henri Desfosse, violet. All repay hard pruning each April as a result of which they will make strong growths 6 to 8 feet in length, terminated by fine sprays of blooms. Perle Rose is one of the few kinds with pale rose instead of blue flowers. On the whole, these deciduous kinds are hardier than the evergreens.

The evergreen species and hybrids need not be pruned annually unless this is necessary to keep them in shape on a wall. Then it is best done immediately after flowering with the May- and early June-flowering kinds, but pruning of those kinds that flower in summer must be done in April.

All kinds of ceanothus can be increased by cuttings from young growth in summer in a propagating frame or under mist.

CELASTRUS Vigorous twiners, grown for their fruits and seeds in autumn. The fruits are the size of large peas and are green outside, but when they ripen they split open to reveal large scarlet seeds imbedded in an orange-yellow matrix. When the fruits are freely produced this is a very handsome sight comparable with that of the Spindle Trees. Unfortunately celastrus does not always fruit freely and it has little else to offer. The explanation is that *Celastrus orbiculatus*, the species commonly grown, is normally a unisexual plant, *i.e.*, female and male flowers are borne on separate plants. The berries are only produced by the female flowers and then only when fertilised by pollen from male flowers. It is necessary, therefore, to plant both sexes unless the hermaphrodite form, with flowers of both sexes on the same plant, can be obtained.

C. orbiculatus is a vigorous plant, capable of covering quite large tree stumps or ascending living trees. It makes a useful cover for outhouses and unsightly buildings, though it is deciduous and will not give any cover in winter. It will

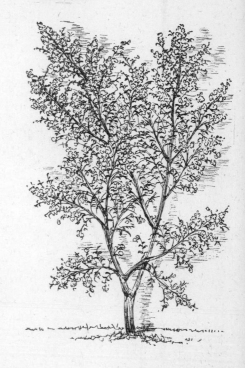

Ceanothus veitchianus

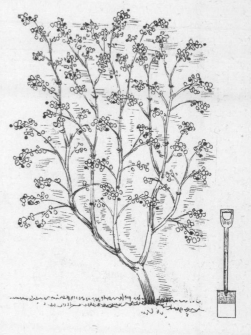

Celastrus orbiculatus

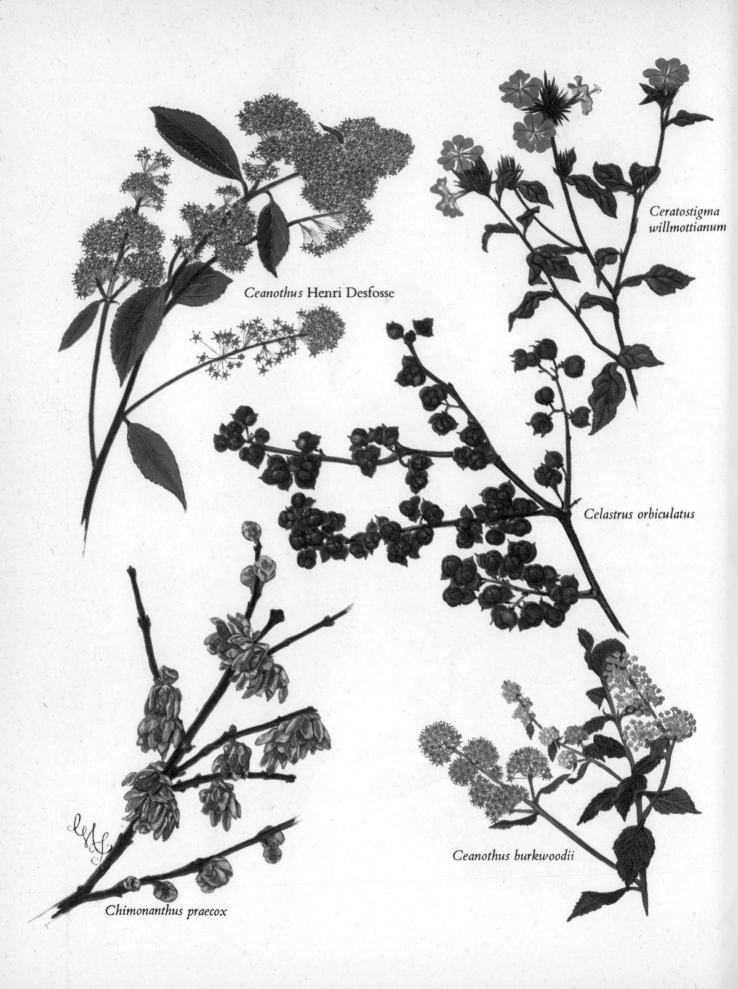

Ceratostigma willmottianum

Ceanothus Henri Desfosse

Celastrus orbiculatus

Chimonanthus praecox

Ceanothus burkwoodii

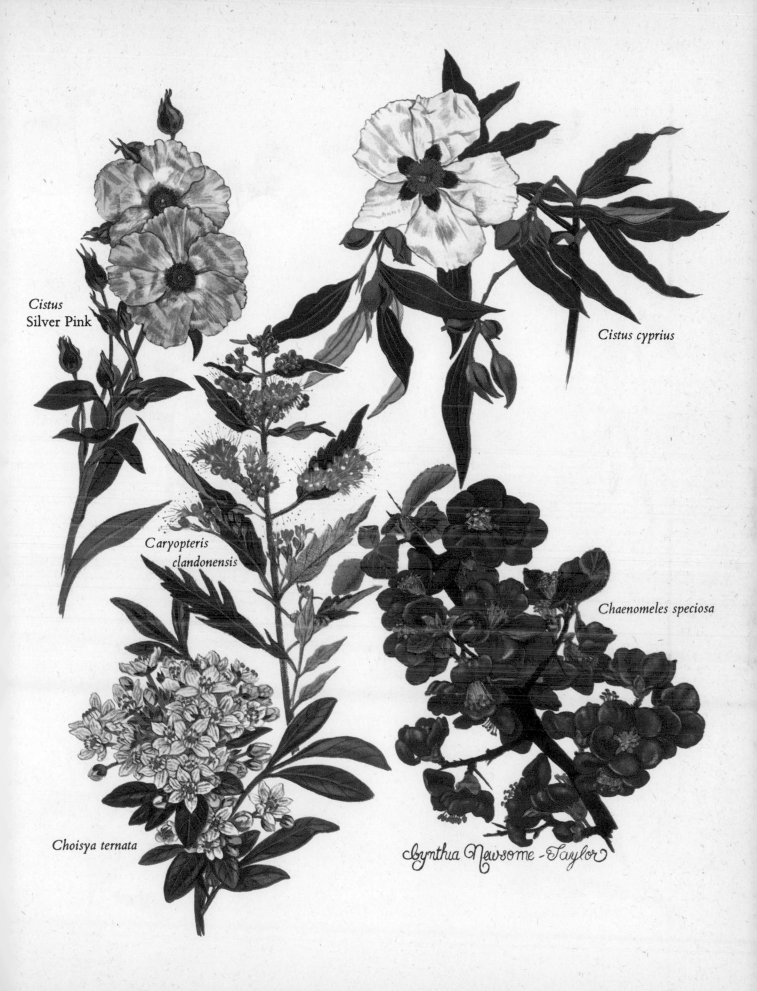

Cistus
Silver Pink

Cistus cyprius

Caryopteris clandonensis

Chaenomeles speciosa

Choisya ternata

Cynthia Newsome-Taylor

Ceratostigma willmottianum

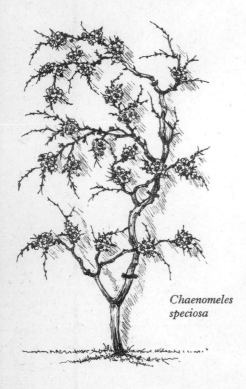

Chaenomeles speciosa

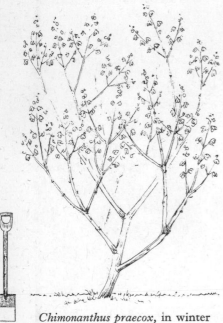

Chimonanthus praecox, in winter

grow in almost any soil except those that are very poor and needs no regular pruning, but excessive growth can be cut out in winter.

Propagation is by seeds sown in a frame or greenhouse in spring, or young stems may be layered in spring or early summer.

CERATOSTIGMA The species commonly grown, *Ceratostigma willmottianum*, though truly a shrub, is often cut back to ground level by frost in winter, so that it behaves like a herbaceous plant, dying down and then shooting up again the following spring. It is a beautiful and useful plant, producing plenty of bright blue, phlox-like flowers from July to October. It will reach a height of 2 feet, more if it is not cut down, and gradually spread over several square feet of ground. It likes a warm, sunny situation and good well-drained soil. Any pruning necessary to get rid of dead or damaged growth should be left until April as the old growth, even when dead, serves as some protection against frost for the roots and basal buds. There is another shrubby species, *C. griffithii*, but it is rare and more tender.

Propagation of both these shrubby species of *Ceratostigma* is by cuttings of firm young growth in summer in a propagating frame or under mist.

CHAENOMELES (Flowering Quince, Japonica) This is the genus that was once called *Cydonia* by botanists and still is by most gardeners. To add to the confusion, the names of the two most popular species have also been changed, so that what most gardeners and many nursery catalogues still call *Cydonia japonica* we must learn to call *Chaenomeles speciosa* and what used to be *Cydonia maulei* becomes *Chaenomeles japonica*. *C. speciosa* is the familiar Japanese Quince, popular as a wall-trained shrub, with scarlet blossom coming with the forsythia in March. Planted in the open, and left to its own devices, it will make a densely spiny bush, 6 feet high and as much or more through. Against a wall, it must be pruned and trained to make it fill the required space.

In addition to the familiar scarlet-flowered variety, there are others with flowers of different colours and forms, white in *nivalis*, pink and white in *moerloesii*, pink and double in *rosea flore pleno*, scarlet and double in *sanguinea plena*. More names will be found in nursery catalogues, but these tend to differ from firm to firm as it is easy to raise the Japanese quince from seed and seedlings show many colour variations.

Chaenomeles japonica is a much shorter plant, rarely above 3 feet in height though it may have a spread of 8 or 9 feet. Typically, all flowers are orange-scarlet, but again there are variations chiefly, I think, as a result of crosses, accidental or by design, with *C. speciosa*. In some nursery catalogues these hybrid forms may be listed separately under the name *C. superba*. Two are of special note—Knap Hill Scarlet for the size and brilliance of its orange-scarlet flowers, and *simonii* for its semi-double blood-red flowers.

All chaenomeles are deciduous, quite hardy and easily grown in almost any soil. They flower most freely in full sun but will grow in partial shade. When grown as bushes no pruning is necessary, but trained against a wall some thinning out is best as soon as the flowers fade. At the same time, forward-pointing stems can be cut back to 2 or 3 inches.

An easy way of providing a few extra plants is to dig up suckers with roots any time between October and March. Where more plants are required chaenomeles can be increased by layering in late spring or early summer.

CHIMONANTHUS (Winter Sweet) The flowers of *Chimonanthus praecox*, the only species cultivated, are not showy, but they come in mid-winter and will perfume the air for yards around. This shrub is deciduous, has a rather open habit and is best trained against a wall, preferably one facing south or west. It will grow 8 to 10 feet in height and rather more through and the flowers, which have a rather waxy texture, are very pale primrose marked with purple at the centre. A variety, named *grandiflorus*, has larger flowers and another, named *luteus*, lacks the purple marking.

No chimonanthus is completely hardy except in the milder parts of the country—hence the desirability of planting against a sheltered wall. All varieties like a good loamy well-drained soil. The only pruning required is the removal or shortening of surplus or badly placed stems, which is best done after flowering.

Propagation is by layering in spring or early summer.

CHOISYA (Mexican Orange Blossom) The only species grown, *Choisya ternata*, is a handsome evergreen with clusters of white, fragrant flowers, rather like orange blossom. The main flush of flowers comes in May but choisya will go on flowering spasmodically for a long time after that. The leaves are a light shining green, the bush is well branched and dome-like in habit and in favourable places may reach a height and spread of 7 or 8 feet, but is usually more like 5 or 6 feet. It has a reputation for tenderness though with me it has survived quite severe frost without protection. I do think, however, that it should be given a place sheltered from north and east winds and some extra protection, such as a sacking screen, the first winter after planting. No regular pruning is required.

Choisya ternata

Propagation is by cuttings of firm young growth in summer, reared in a propagating frame or under mist. Autumn cuttings will also root, but more slowly, in an unheated frame.

CISTUS (Rock Rose) These very beautiful evergreen shrubs are none too hardy and losses were heavy in the severe winter of 1962-63, but they are so readily raised from seeds or cuttings and grow so quickly, even in the poorest soils, that some risk can be accepted. However, in cold districts I would only recommend planting the hardiest, or perhaps more accurately, the least tender, kinds. These, in my experience are *Cistus crispus*, a compact 2-foot bush with rose flowers; *C. corbariensis*, 3-foot high and rather more through, with white flowers; *C. laurifolius*, a much taller and broader plant, to 6 feet in favourable places, with all-white flowers; and *C. cyprius*, similar in growth to the last with white flowers blotched with maroon.

One of the most handsome is *C. purpureus*, with very large rose-coloured flowers blotched with maroon. It is usually about 4 feet high and 4 or 5 feet through but will grow larger in favourable places. *C.* Silver Pink has smaller flowers, soft pink without blotches, and is particularly beautiful. It averages 3 feet high and 4 feet through. *C. lusitanicus* has large white flowers blotched with maroon and grows to 5 or 6 feet, but it has a spreading form named *C. l. prostratus* which does not often exceed 2 feet though it may spread to 4 or 5 feet. *C. ladaniferus* is known as the Gum Cistus because its leaves are sticky with gum. The leaves of several species are pleasantly aromatic but *C. ladaniferus* excells in this respect. It grows to 5 feet, is a little broader than this and has large white flowers.

Cistus cyprius

All Rock Roses like light, well-drained soils and sunny positions and most are first-class seaside shrubs. They should, if possible, be given shelter from North and East as cold winds can defoliate them. No regular pruning is necessary.

Propagation is by seed sown in a greenhouse or frame in spring or by cuttings of firm young growth in summer in a propagating frame or under mist.

CLEMATIS No genus has provided gardens with a greater range and variety of climbing plants than this. So important has it become, partly through the introduction of more and more species but even more as a result of hybridisation and garden selection, that several books have been devoted to the clematis.

It is difficult to generalise about so varied a group of plants. Our native species *Clematis vitalba*, popularly known as Traveller's Joy or Old Man's Beard, is always found growing wild on limestone or chalk. This has led to the belief that all kinds of clematis are lime lovers, but it would almost certainly be more true to say that, while all will tolerate lime, most will thrive on any soil that is in reasonable condition and not liable to dry out badly in summer.

Another dangerous generalisation is that all clematis are liable to die suddenly and mysteriously, often after they have been happily established for years. This is certainly true of a good many of the large-flowered garden hybrids but I have

Cistus purpureus

Clematis macropetala

Clematis jackman
Perle d'Azur

Clematis patens
Lasurstern

Clematis viticella
Etoile Violette

Clematis viticella
Ville de Lyon

Clematis tangutica

Clematis texensis
Gravetye Beauty

Cynthia Newsome-Taylor

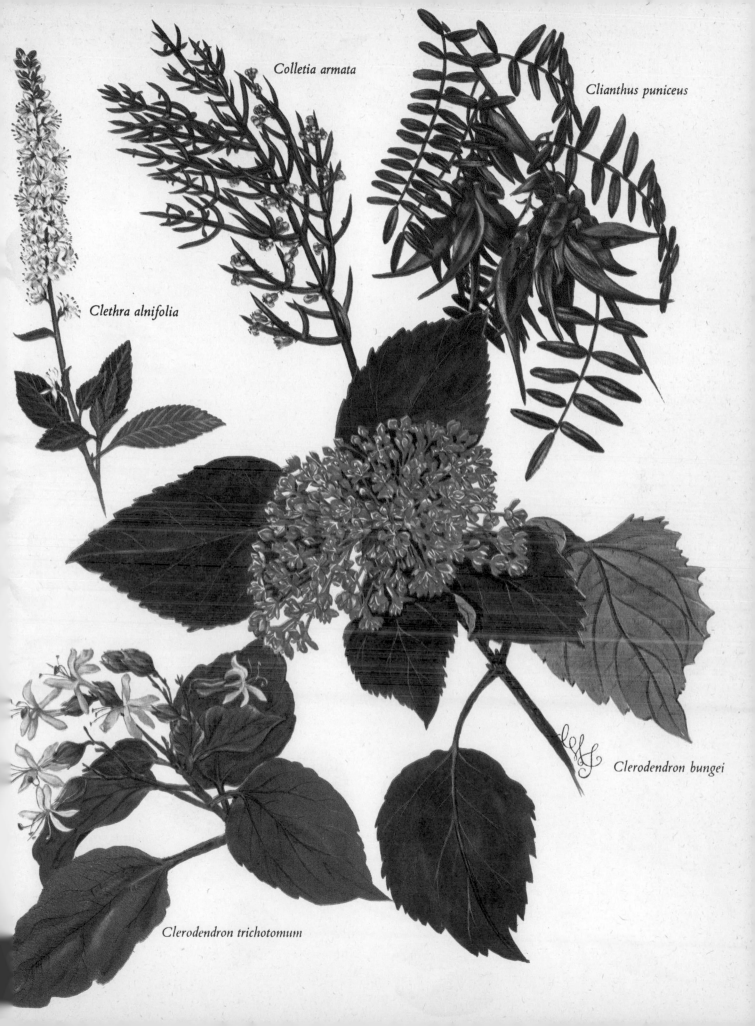

Colletia armata

Clianthus puniceus

Clethra alnifolia

Clerodendron bungei

Clerodendron trichotomum

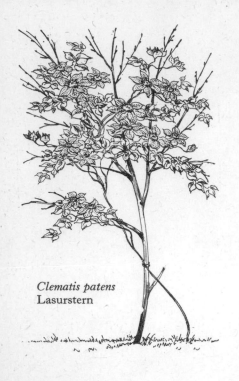

Clematis patens
Lasurstern

Clematis florida
sieboldii

Clerodendron bungei

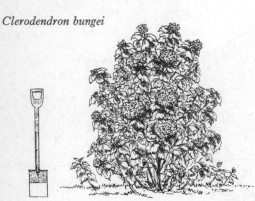

never observed any tendency to sudden death in the smaller-flowered species such as *C. montana*, *C. flammula* and *C. tangutica*.

Most clematis are deciduous, but a few are evergreen and one of these, *C. armandii*, is hardy enough to be grown outdoors in all except the coldest districts. It is a fairly vigorous climber with large leathery leaves and clusters of white flowers in April. It does not climb so securely as some and needs a fair amount of tying if it is not to be dislodged by gales.

Clematis montana is much more rampant, capable of reaching 20 feet or more and covering a considerable area with its dense growth. Typically the flowers, which come in May, are white but there are pink forms, of which *C. montana rubens* is a good example.

Clematis macropetala is a much more fragile plant with clusters of nodding lavender-blue flowers in May. Late in the summer comes *C. flammula* with cloud-like clusters of small white flowers and *C. tangutica* with yellow flowers, the petals curled to form a little hood. Another yellow-flowered species, flowering at the same time, is *C. orientalis*. *C. florida* is usually represented by its semi-double variety, *C. florida sieboldii*, with purple and white flowers.

The garden hybrids mostly have larger flowers. One of the oldest, most popular and still among the best is *C. jackmanii*, with violet-purple flowers in July and August. Its flowers are of finest quality if the plant is pruned fairly severely each March, either being cut back to within a foot or so of ground level or, if it is to cover a greater space, having all its younger growths cut back to within a few inches of a main framework of more mature vines.

Other very popular garden varieties are *C. henryi*, with very large white flowers in June and July; Nelly Moser, with big, pale mauve flowers, banded with purple; Comtesse de Bouchard, soft pink; Lasurstern, purple-blue, Perle d'Azur, light blue; Etiole Violette, deep purple; Ville de Lyon, carmine red; and Gravetye Beauty, deep red. The names of many more will be found in catalogues.

Clematis transplants rather badly and plants are best purchased in pots from which they can be transferred with a minimum of root disturbance. They can be planted at any time from September to May. The more vigorous species and hybrids may be placed where they can scramble up into old fruit trees or over shrubs, but the choicer varieties are best grown up trellis work or on wires against walls. Avoid planting where roots will get baked by direct sunshine. Herbaceous plants or small shrubs may be grown in front to shade them, but not very vigorous kinds that might rob them of too much food and moisture.

The large-flowered garden hybrids will appreciate some rotted manure or compost in the soil before planting and an annual spring mulch of manure or compost. Most will also benefit from pruning in March, when weak growth can be shortened or cut out, but the early-flowering kinds (*e.g.*, *C. armandii*, *C. macropetala* and *C. montana*) should not be pruned until after flowering.

All clematis can be increased by layering in spring or early summer. Cuttings of many kinds will root in summer in sand in a propagating frame or under mist. All the species can be raised from seed sown in a greenhouse or frame in spring. Seed from large-flowered varieties can also give interesting results, though the seedlings may not closely resemble their parents.

CLERODENDRON Two species, both deciduous, are cultivated and are valuable for their late flowering, but both suffer the disadvantage of having leaves which give off a heavy repulsive smell when bruised. They need to be planted where they can be seen but not inadvertently touched.

Clerodendron bungei will grow 5 to 6 feet high and as much or more through, but as it is rather tender and often cut back to ground level by frost, it may not attain these dimensions in cold gardens. The leaves are large, dark green above and covered with reddish hairs beneath. The small flowers are purplish rose, crowded into rounded heads 5 or 6 inches across. They appear in August and September.

The other species, *C. trichotomum*, is a bigger plant, more woody and loosely branched, often 10 feet high and as much or more through. The flowers are pleasantly fragrant, white with brownish-red calices which persist after the petals have fallen and then surround the small turquoise berries. It has a variety, sometimes listed as a separate species, named *fargesii*, with smooth instead of downy leaves. Some gardeners consider that it berries more freely than the type and that it is hardier.

Because of their doubtful hardiness, clerodendrons should be given a sunny sheltered place, *C. bungei* even more so than *C. trichotomum*. Neither is fussy as regards soil. The only pruning required is the removal, in spring, of stems killed or damaged by frost.

As both species sucker freely, removal of rooted suckers in autumn usually provides the amateur with all the plants he requires but both species can also be increased by summer cuttings in a frame with soil warming and by seed sown in a greenhouse or frame in spring.

CLETHRA In America, where it grows wild, *Clethra alnifolia* is called the Summer Sweet or Sweet Pepperbush because of the strong aromatic perfume of its slender spikes of small white flowers. It is the best species for cultivation in British gardens, but it requires a cool, rather moist acid soil, preferably with some peat or leafmould. It will grow 7 or 8 feet high and rather more through. The branches arch pleasingly and the flowers appear in August. A form, known as *paniculata*, is superior in bloom but otherwise differs little. There is also a form with pink flowers.

No regular pruning is required. Propagation is by cuttings of firm young growth in summer in a close frame or under mist; by layering in spring or early summer, or by seed sown in a frame or greenhouse in spring. It is also sometimes possible to dig out rooted suckers in autumn.

CLIANTHUS (Lobster Claw, Parrot's Bill) Only one species is really suitable for planting outdoors in Britain and even this needs the protection of a sunny sheltered wall in all except the mildest districts. This is *Clianthus puniceus*, a trailing or sprawling shrub which looks best trained up a wall. The leaves are made up of a number of small leaflets in the manner of so many of the pea family to which this plant belongs though the flowers have little superficial resemblance to those of a pea. This is because the keel petals are extended to form a kind of beak or claw, a peculiarity which gives this plant its two popular names. In the common form the flower is scarlet, but there is a white-flowered variety.

Clianthus puniceus is evergreen in a very mild winter, but usually in Britain loses all or most of its leaves. It is not a very strong climber but will reach a height of 6 or 7 feet. It flowers in July and August. No pruning is required, except to remove, in spring, growth damaged or killed in winter. Cuttings of firm young growth will root in summer in a propagating frame or under mist, preferably with soil warming.

COLLETIA These very curious shrubs are heavily armed with thick, sometimes flattened, branchlets that are sharply pointed at the tip. Often the plants are quite leafless, the branches serving as leaves, but if leaves are produced they are very small and may pass unnoticed.

The species most commonly seen is *Colletia cruciata* which has triangular branchlets set rigidly on the branches. The flowers are small white or pale pink pitchers, produced very freely in late summer and autumn.

Two other species occasionally grown are *C. infausta* (often wrongly called *C. spinosa*) which has cylindrical branchlet-spines and greenish-white flowers in April and May, and *C. armata* which also has cylindrical spines but produces its white flowers in autumn.

Colletias are not difficult to grow and all appear reasonably hardy. They are not fussy regarding soil, should be given a sunny position and need no pruning. Propagation is by seed sown in a warm greenhouse in spring or by summer cuttings in a propagating frame or under mist.

COLUTEA (Bladder Senna) Were it not for their large seed pods, like inflated parchment bladders, the coluteas might be considered rather unexciting

Clethra alnifolia

Colletia armata

Clianthus puniceus

Colutea arborescens
(flowers)

Convolvulus cneorum

Colutea arborescens
(fruit)

Cornus alba spaethii

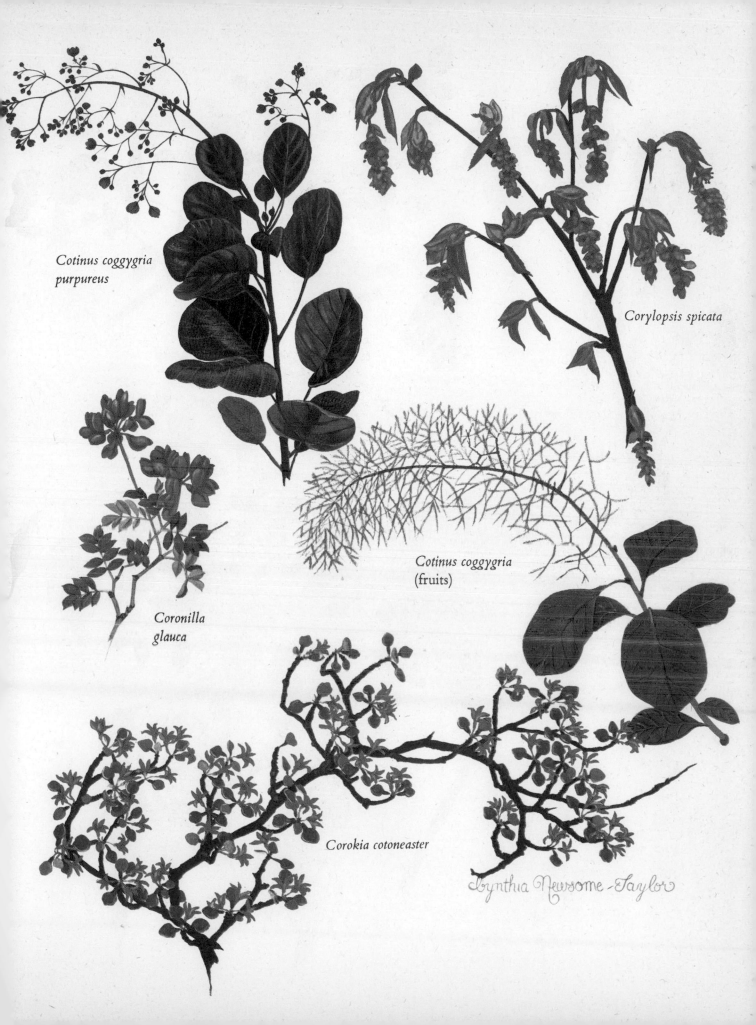

Cotinus coggygria
purpureus

Corylopsis spicata

Coronilla
glauca

Cotinus coggygria
(fruits)

Corokia cotoneaster

Cynthia Newsome-Taylor

*Colutea
arborescens*

Cornus alba spaethii

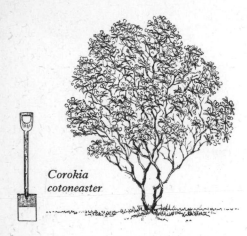

*Corokia
cotoneaster*

shrubs. Their pea-type flowers are not quite large enough or sufficiently freely produced, though they have the merit of coming over a long season, roughly from June to October. But the seed vessels are attractive as well as curious.

The species most commonly planted is *Colutea arborescens* which will grow to 10 or 12 feet high and through but can be kept a good deal smaller by pruning each February or March. It has yellow flowers. *C. orientalis* is only about half the height and spread and has brownish-red flowers and grey foliage, and there is a hybrid between the two, named *C. media*, which is intermediate in height and colour.

All are very easy to grow in almost any soil and in open situations. They are easily increased by seed, sown in spring in a frame or greenhouse, or even outdoors in a sheltered place, or by cuttings of firm young growth in summer in a frame or under mist.

CONVOLVULUS Most of the species of convolvulus are herbaceous plants or annuals and several are troublesome weeds, but one is an excellent small shrub, useful for the rock garden or the extreme front of the shrub border. This is *Convolvulus cneorum*, a neat bush usually about 2 feet high and through with silvery leaves and funnel-shaped flowers, white flushed with pink, produced during most of the summer. It is none too hardy and survives best in light sandy soils and sunny, sheltered places. It is easily raised from cuttings of firm young growths in summer in a propagating frame, preferably with bottom heat, and it is as well to strike a few cuttings annually and keep the plants in a frame or greenhouse during the winter in case plants should be killed by frost.

CORNUS (Dogwood) Many of the most beautiful kinds, such as *Cornus florida*, *C. kousa* and *C. nuttallii*, are trees and therefore outside the range of this book. But there are some genuinely shrubby kinds the most generally useful of which is *C. alba* in its several fine forms. This cornus grows 7 or 8 feet high and 9 or 10 feet through. Its flowers are small, yellowish-white and not very decorative, the shrub being grown for its red bark. This is particularly colourful on the year-old stems and the best way to enjoy this shrub is to cut it almost to ground level each March, so making it throw up a thicket of young growth. But for bark colour it is surpassed by the variety *sibirica* (sometimes called *atrosanguinea*), the Westonbirt Dogwood. There is also a form of this known as *C. alba sibirica variegata*, with silver edges to the leaves, a very attractive shrub with the same light red bark. This must no be confused with another fine variegated dogwood, *C. alba spaethii*, in which the variegation is yellow and the red colour of the bark less brilliant. To complicate nomenclature still more there is a third variety, named *C. alba variegata*, which has silver variegation but the red bark is not as brilliant as that of *C. alba sibirica variegata*.

Another desirable shrubby Dogwood is *C. stolonifera* which has deep red bark and spreads freely by suckers. There is a variety of this, named *flaviramea*, which has bright yellow bark and makes a fine companion for any of the red-barked Dogwoods. *C. stolonifera* and its variety should also be cut back each spring to see its bark colour to full advantage.

These are all easily grown shrubs thriving in most soils and seen to particular advantage near the waterside. They are all easily raised from cuttings of ripe growth in autumn, inserted outdoors, or by digging up rooted suckers or layers at any time in autumn or winter.

COROKIA Only one species is commonly grown in gardens, *Corokia cotoneaster*, a rather odd, but distinctly attractive shrub with curiously twisted branches, small leaves and little starry yellow flowers scattered along the branches in May. It will reach a height of 8 feet and spread of 6 feet in favourable circumstances but is usually a good deal less. It is none too hardy and needs a sheltered situation in all but the mildest districts but is not fussy about soil. No pruning is required. Propagation is by cuttings of firm young growth in summer in a propagating frame or under mist with soil warming.

CORONILLA Like so many shrubby members of the pea family, all the coronillas have dainty leaves, composed of numerous small leaflets. Of the species commonly seen in gardens two, *Coronilla emerus* and *C. emeroides*, are deciduous and one, *C. glauca*, is evergreen and distinctly tender, needing the protection of a sunny wall except in the mildest parts of the country.

Coronilla emerus has rather slender, sprawling stems, but will eventually build up a loose mound of growth as much as 6 feet high and even more through. The flowers are yellow and dull red, small, but freely produced from about May to September. *C. emeroides* is similar in appearance but the flowers are yellow throughout. They, too, are produced throughout the summer. In a favourable place *C. glauca* is seldom entirely without some of its yellow flowers. It is most attractive against a wall where it can be trained to a height of 9 or 10 feet. In the open it will make a loose bush 7 or 8 feet high and as much or more through if it is not cut back by frost.

All coronillas like well-drained soils and warm, sunny places. No pruning is required except when *C. glauca* is trained against walls, when badly placed growth can be cut out each spring.

Propagation is by cuttings of firm young growth in summer in a propagating frame or under mist, preferably with soil warming.

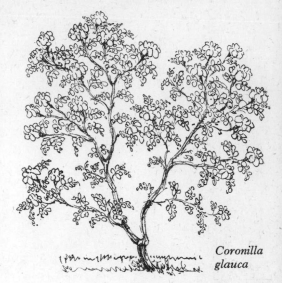

Coronilla glauca

CORYLOPSIS (Winter Hazel) These are for the most part fairly large shrubs, allied to the Witch Hazels. All have soft yellow flowers and most produce these in little pendant trails in March and April. Of this character are *Corylopsis spicata*, which will reach a height and spread of 6 feet; *C. platypetala*, which will go to 8 feet; and *C. willmottiae*, which may reach 12 feet. Quite distinct from these is *C. pauciflora*, which has flowers individually rather larger but clustered in twos or threes instead of hanging in trails. It does not as a rule exceed 4 feet in height and spread.

All will grow in most soils and in sun or partial shade but all are a little tender, especially in flower and young leaf, and so it is wise to give them a fairly sheltered place. They thrive well in thin woodland which will provide the shelter they need. No regular pruning is required. Propagation is by cuttings of firm young growth in summer in a frame or under mist, or by layering in spring or autumn.

COTINUS (Wig Tree, Smoke Plant) The two species of *Cotinus* are highly decorative and distinctive deciduous shrubs, both of which were formerly known as *Rhus* and may still be found under that name in many catalogues and gardens. *Cotinus coggygria* was formerly known as *Rhus cotinus* and is a big bush, 10 to 12 feet high, spreading by suckers so that its eventual width is indeterminate. Its leaves turn yellow, orange and crimson in autumn and are preceded by extraordinary flowers, small and inconspicuous in themselves but with slender hairy stalks which lengthen into silky filaments, at first pinkish-brown, later grey. It is the tangled masses of these that have prompted the popular names Wig Tree and Smoke Plant. A variety named *purpureus* has leaves which are purple throughout. The other species, *C. americanus*, also known as *C. cotinoides* and as *Rhus cotinoides*, has smaller leaves and even more brilliant autumn colour, but is nothing like so effective in flower. It will reach 20 feet.

Both species like well-drained soils and open sunny positions. No pruning is required. They can usually be increased by suckers dug up with roots in autumn or winter, but failing these stems can be layered in spring or early summer.

Cotinus coggygria purpureus

COTONEASTER This is one of the really big shrub families with many species, some of which hybridise easily and almost all of which have some decorative merit. The berries, usually red or crimson but black in a few kinds, are a conspicuous autumn feature. Some cotoneasters are evergreen, some deciduous, some are bushy shrubs, others low growing, spreading or even prostrate.

Taking the deciduous kinds first, *Cotoneaster adpressus* is one of the most prostrate, *C. frigidus* one of the tallest—too tall perhaps to be regarded as shrub at all. *C. adpressus* rarely rises more than a foot above the ground but may spread

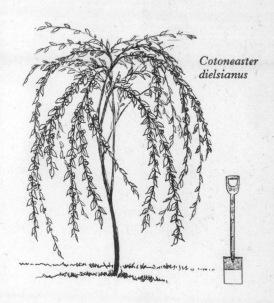

Cotoneaster dielsianus

Cotoneaster dielsianus

Cotoneaster *horizontalis*

Cotoneaster conspicuus
decorus

Cotoneaster Cornubia

Cytisus albus

Cytisus praecox

Cytisus scoparius andreanus

Cytisus battandieri

Cynthia Newsome Taylor

Cotoneaster conspicuus

Cotoneaster horizontalis

Cotoneaster Cornubia

for several yards. It has small leaves which turn red before they fall and, for a time, add to the effect of the red berries, which persist longer. By contrast *C. frigidus* has leaves 4 or 5 inches long, big hanging clusters of red berries and it may reach 25 feet under favourable conditions. This is one of the most handsome species in flower, as the white flowers are produced very freely in late May in quite large, hanging clusters.

Between these extremes, three species and one hybrid may serve to illustrate the deciduous section of the family. They are *C. horizontalis*, *C. simonsii*, *C. dielsianus*, and *C.* Cornubia.

Cotoneaster horizontalis is the well-known Herring-bone or Fish-bone Cotoneaster, so called from the regular fish-bone-like arrangement of its branches. Planted in the open it will grow about 3 feet high and in time may spread to 9 or 10 feet. Planted against a wall it will fan out and ascend to a height of 6 or 8 feet without support. The berries are bright red and the neat, shining green leaves also turn red before falling. There is a pretty variety with silver variegated leaves.

Cotoneaster simonsii grows rather stiffly erect and will reach a height of 10 feet, though it is unlikely to be more than 8 feet through. It can easily be kept a lot smaller by pruning in spring or early summer. It makes an excellent hedge plant and in a mild winter will retain many leaves for most of the time. The berries are scarlet and hang a long time.

Cotoneaster dielsianus is much more graceful in habit, with long slender, arching branches and little clusters of deep red berries. It will reach a height of 8 or 9 feet and a spread of 9 or 10 feet. Under some conditions it may be evergreen and this is particularly likely in the variety named *elegans*. *C.* Cornubia is a hybrid, perhaps with *C. frigidus* as one of its parents. It is very strong growing and its scarlet berries are particularly large and showy.

The evergreen cotoneasters have just as wide a range, indeed the most prostrate shrub of the whole genus, *C. dammeri*, is an evergreen. This hugs the ground, or any rocks it may encounter on its way, and makes good cover for banks. It will spread for yards, rooting as it goes. The berries are bright red.

Cotoneaster microphyllus is an evergreen match for *C. horizontalis*, but more rounded in habit, about 3 foot high, with very small dark green leaves and deep red berries. It is a good plant to drape over a low wall. Both *C. buxifolius* and *C. congestus* are closely akin to *C. microphyllus* but the latter is shorter in branch, denser in growth and more suitable for the rock garden whereas *C. buxifolius* is more vigorous and has larger leaves.

Cotoneaster conspicuus is taller still, a dense rounded mound of growth as much as 5 feet high. The leaves are small and rounded, the berries orange-scarlet, very freely produced. There is a shorter form of this known as *decorus*.

Cotoneaster franchetii is quite different in habit from any of the foregoing evergreens, a loosely-branched, graceful bush 8 to 10 feet high and through with lance-shaped leaves and orange-red berries. *C. salicifolius* is even taller, with longer, narrower leaves and a similar open habit. It has a useful prostrate form which can be planted on banks or as ground cover.

Cotoneaster lacteus has oval leaves of firm, almost leathery, texture and orange-red berries that hang a long time. It is 10 to 12 feet in height and diameter. *C. watereri* is a fine hybrid between the deciduous *C. frigidus* and the evergreen *C. henryanus*. It has inherited great vigour from one parent, graceful habit from the other and produces scarlet berries with the greatest freedom. It is evergreen or nearly so.

All these cotoneasters are easily grown in practically any soil. They flower and fruit most freely in sunny places but will grow in shade. No regular pruning is essential but all can be pruned if it is necessary to restrict their size, and this is best done in March or April.

All the species can be raised from seed sown in a frame or outdoors in spring and self-sown seedlings often appear around plants. The hybrids will not come true from seed, though they may give interesting seedlings. All can be increased by cuttings of firm young growth in summer in a propagating frame or under mist, or from cuttings of ripe growth in autumn in an ordinary frame or sheltered place outdoors.

CYTISUS (Broom) Many of the popular garden varieties of broom are either varieties of *Cytisus scoparius*, the Common Yellow Broom, or are hybrids between this and *C. albus* (also known as *C. multiflorus*), the White Portugal Broom. *C. scoparius* is native to Britain, an erect plant to 10 feet high and through, with bright yellow flowers in its typical form but with varieties more or less heavily splashed with orange or crimson. *C. albus* is just as tall, rather narrower and has thinner whippier stems and smaller but more numerous white flowers. The garden varieties and hybrids give a very wide colour range from cream to deepest yellow, soft rose to crimson with some showing delightful combinations of colours—crimson and yellow in Firefly, rose and cream in Donard Seedling and cerise and maroon in *burkwoodii*. All flower in May.

Cytisus praecox

In addition there are many other species which further extend the range and garden usefulness of the brooms. *C. procumbens* sprawls about, making a mat of thin stems covered with yellow flowers in May. It is only a few inches high but may cover several feet of ground. *C. ardoinii* is a little taller but much more compact, a tufted bushlet 5 or 6 inches high with bright yellow flowers in late April or early May. It is an excellent rock garden shrub. So is *C. beanii*, a rather taller hybrid between *C. ardoinii* and a 3-foot tall species, seldom seen in gardens, named *C. purgans*.

Cytisus ardoinii crossed with *C. albus* has given *C. kewensis*, which sprays its stems out sideways and smothers them in May with cream flowers. *C. albus* crossed with *C. purgans* has produced another very popular broom, *C. praecox*, which will reach 6 or 7 feet in time but has arching branches inherited from *C. purgans*. The cream flowers come in April.

C. purpureus is another of the sprawlers, not much over a foot high but spreading a long way aided by suckers thrown up from the roots. The flowers, in May, are purplish-rose or lilac. *C. nigricans* flowers later than most, in July and August. The flowers are yellow and the bush 3 to 4 feet high and through.

Cytisus battandieri is very different in appearance from all the foregoing, a shrub of open habit, 12 to 15 feet high and even more through, with quite large, silvery leaves and erect spikes of yellow pineapple-scented flowers in July.

Cytisus battandieri

All these brooms are easily grown once established but they tend to be difficult to move and are often rather short-lived. They thrive best and live longest on fairly light, well-drained soils but they can be grown on almost all soils. All are sun lovers.

Because of their dislike of root disturbance, nurserymen usually grow young plants in pots so that they can be moved with roots and soil intact. The larger kinds may need staking at first to prevent them being blown about but, once established, they should be able to support themselves. They are good seaside shrubs.

Pruning of the small kinds is seldom necessary but the larger kinds, and particularly the garden forms of *C. scoparius*, benefit from light cutting back after flowering. They must not be cut back into old wood, which is seldom capable of producing new growth. Simply shorten by two-thirds or three-quarters the whippy young stems, most of which will actually be carrying faded flowers at the time of pruning.

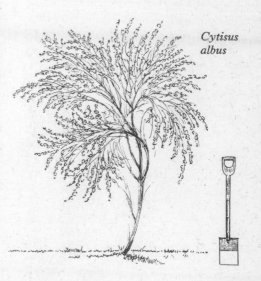

Cytisus albus

Seed provides an easy way of increase, but the garden varieties do not come true to colour. For this reason selected garden varieties must be increased by cuttings or by grafting on to seedling brooms or seedling laburnum. Seed can be sown as soon as it is ripe or in early spring outdoors or in a frame or unheated greenhouse. Seedlings are best potted individually at an early stage and grown on in pots until they are large enough for their permanent positions. Cuttings are taken in July or August and are best rooted under mist. Grafting is done in spring under glass on to seedling broom or laburnum. Brooms, such as *C. purpureus*, which spread by suckers can be increased by digging up rooted suckers at any time between October and April.

Daphne cneorum eximia

Daphne burkwoodii

Daphne mezereum

Daboecia cantabrica

Danaë racemosa

Daboecia cantabrica alba

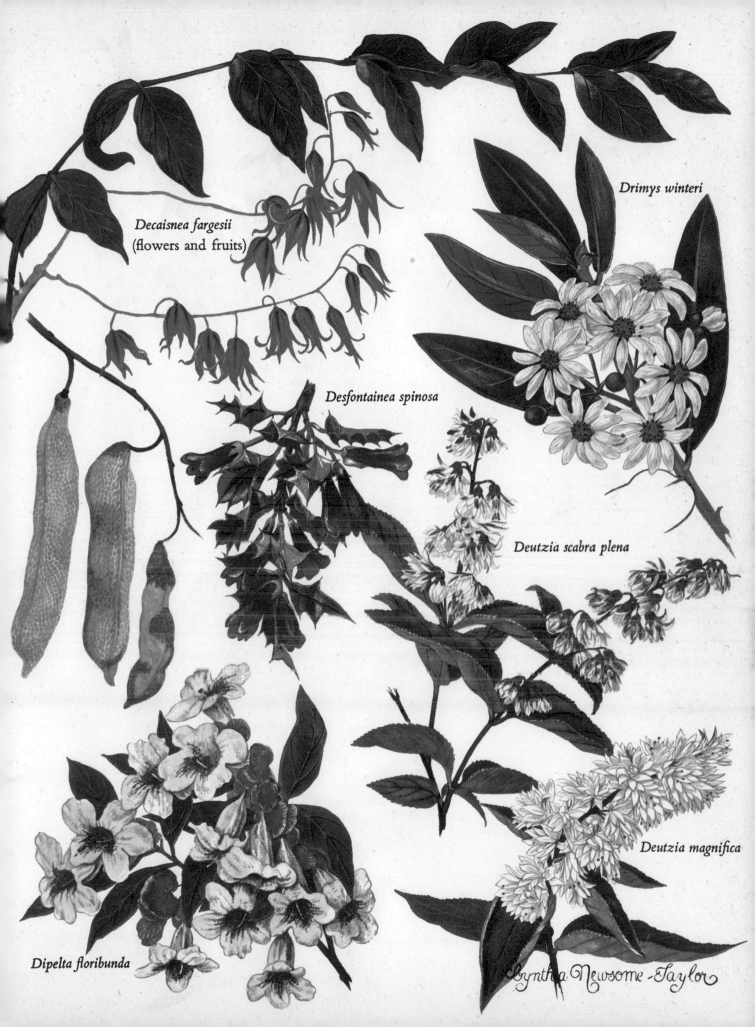

Decaisnea fargesii
(flowers and fruits)

Drimys winteri

Desfontainea spinosa

Deutzia scabra plena

Deutzia magnifica

Dipelta floribunda

Cynthia Newsome-Taylor

Daboecia cantabrica

Daphne cneorum eximia

Daphne mezereum

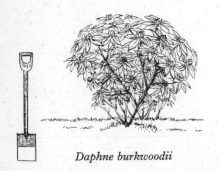

Daphne burkwoodii

DABOECIA (Irish Heath) Only one species is commonly grown, *Daboecia cantabrica*, often known in gardens as *D. polifolia* and occasionally as *Menziesia polifolia*. It looks like a heather and belongs to the heather family. It grows about 2 feet high and through, has narrow leaves and sprays of little bell-like flowers, purple in the common form and white in the variety *alba*. There is also a variety, named *bicolor*, which carries white and purple flowers on the same plant and another, named *praegerae*, which has pink flowers. All flower from June to October. One other species occasionally seen is *D. azorica*, about 1 foot high and through, with crimson flowers. It is slightly tender and only suitable for sheltered places.

All require exactly the same conditions as heather, *i.e.* well-drained lime-free soils, preferably containing some peat or leafmould. They thrive best in open positions and benefit from a light trimming with shears after flowering.

All can be raised from seed sown on the surface of sandy peat in a frame or cool greenhouse in spring. Selected varieties should be increased by cuttings of firm young shoots in summer in a propagating frame or under mist.

DANAË (Alexandrian Laurel) One species only is grown, *Danaë racemosa*, sometimes known in gardens as *D. laurus* and occasionally as *Ruscus racemosus*. It is closely related to the Butcher's Broom, *Ruscus aculeatus*, and, like it, has flattened stems which function as leaves, but whereas these false leaves are stiff and sharp pointed in the Butcher's Broom, they are soft and unarmed in the Alexandrian Laurel. They are very decorative and cut stems are much in demand as 'foliage' for flower arrangements. The greenish flowers are insignificant.

Danaë racemosa grows about 3 feet tall and slowly spreads by offsets. It thrives in shade, even in dense shade under trees, and it retains its 'leaves' throughout the winter. It is quite hardy and will grown in any reasonable soil. Regular pruning is not essential, but if a few branches are cut from time to time for decorative use the bush will suffer no harm. It can be increased by division or by chopping off rooted offsets any time from October to April.

DAPHNE Some of the most fragrant of all shrubs are included in this genus, which contains both evergreen and deciduous species, some so small that their proper place is the rock garden, some considerably larger and suitable for the shrub border.

Daphne mezereum is one of the most popular, a deciduous shrub flowering on the bare stems in February and March. Typically the flowers are a deep magenta but there is a pure white variety named *alba*. In both the flowers are followed by red berries. This daphne grows about 4 feet high and 3 feet through and tends to be rather short-lived, often dying suddenly when apparently in full health. Frequently it will reproduce itself by self-sown seedlings and it is worth retaining some of these in case the parent should die.

Another popular deciduous daphne is *D. burkwoodii*. This is a hybrid which also passes under the name *D. Somerset*. It is much more branching than *D. mezereum*, about 3 feet high and as much as 5 or 6 feet through. The small pink flowers are intensely fragrant and very freely produced in May.

One of the parents of *D. burkwoodii* is *D. cneorum*, a much shorter plant, seldom much above a foot high but spreading to 3 or 4 feet, evergreen with rose-pink fragrant flowers in May. It looks wonderful at the front of a border or planted in the rock garden. A form of this, known as *eximia*, is even lower growing and has brighter rose flowers.

The first of all to flower is *D. odora*, an evergreen 3 to 4 feet high and nearly twice that through, with reddish-purple flowers, often beginning to open in February. It is reputed to be rather tender but survives quite hard winters if given a sheltered place. There is a form, known as *aureo-marginata*, with a narrow gold band around each leaf which is said to be hardier. This survived the dreadful 1962–63 winter with me in a south-facing border. All forms of *D. odora* have delightfully fragrant flowers.

Daphne collina is admired for its neat habit, blue-green foliage and very fragrant purple flowers in April and May. As it only grows 18 inches high, it can be planted in the rock garden. This is also the proper place for *D. blagayana*, a more or less prostrate shrub with terminal clusters of creamy-white fragrant flowers in May, and also for *D. retusa*, a very slow growing evergreen with fragrant rose-coloured flowers in May.

It is difficult to dogmatise about the cultivation of daphnes for they often seem to thrive in a garden where they are neglected or in which conditions seem wrong, and yet to die in another where they are fussed over and given everything the experts advise. In fact the experts themselves disagree, some saying that they like, others that they dislike, lime. Some kinds are undoubtedly more difficult than others, *D. burkwoodii*, *D. mezereum* and *D. odora*, being among the easier and *D. cneorum*, *D. retusa* and *D. blagayana* among the less easy. All, I think, like good moderately rich soil, plenty of moisture while they are growing in spring and early summer and no stagnant water around their roots in winter. All thrive in open, sunny places. Most dislike root disturbance and are best planted from pots or when fairly young. No pruning is required.

Daphne mezereum is best raised from seed sown as soon as ripe or in March. It will germinate outdoors or may be raised in a frame or greenhouse. Self-sown seedlings often appear in the garden. *D. burkwoodii*, *D. odora* and *D. collina* can all be raised from cuttings of firm young growth in June or July in a propagating frame or under mist. *D. cneorum* and *D. blagayana* are best increased by layering in spring or early summer.

Daphne odora

DECAISNEA The only species cultivated in British gardens, *Decaisnea fargesii*, has handsome leaves, blue-grey beneath, sprays of greenish-yellow flowers and extraordinary blue, sausage-shaped fruits. It is an unusual shrub in every way and certainly worth growing, both for its foliage (individual leaves may be as much as 3 feet long, composed of up to 25 separate leaflets) and for its fruits each 3 or 4 inches in length, blue but covered with a grey bloom, hanging from the branches in clusters. It is erect in habit, up to 10 foot high, but not much more than half as wide. It thrives in good, fairly rich soils and should be kept out of frost pockets and exposed places as the young growth is somewhat tender. No regular pruning is required. Propagation is by seed sown in a frame or greenhouse in spring.

Desfontainea spinosa

DESFONTAINEA An evergreen shrub with holly-like leaves and tubular scarlet and yellow flowers. The only species is *Desfontainea spinosa* and this will eventually make a well-branched bush up to 10 feet in height and 7 or 8 feet through. It is rather tender and is seen to best advantage in south-western and western gardens. The flowers appear from July to October. It likes good, loamy soil and the protection of surrounding shrubs. No pruning is required. Propagation is by seed sown in a warm greenhouse in spring.

DEUTZIA Deciduous shrubs grown for their small but abundant flowers which may be white, pink or purple. There are a number of species and also hybrids and garden varieties. Most popular are *Deutzia scabra* and the varieties derived from it. All these will grow to a height of 10 feet and spread 6 or 7 feet with much the shape of a shuttlecock, but can be kept considerably smaller by pruning. The flowers are produced in June and are white and single in *D. scabra* itself, double tinged with purple outside in *plena* and Pride of Rochester. Closely related to *D. scabra* and probably hybrids from it, are such garden varieties as Mont Rose, rose-pink, Perle Rose, soft rose, and Magician, purplish-pink, all with larger flowers than the wild type. *D. magnifica* also belongs to this group and has quite large cluster of pure white, double flowers.

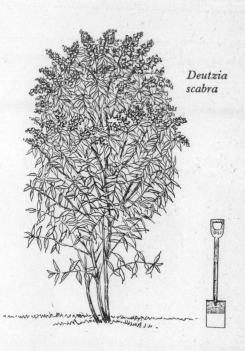

Deutzia scabra

Deutzia purpurascens is a slightly smaller shrub, to 7 feet high and 5 feet through, with flowers which are white inside and purple without. Like *D. scabra* it flowers in June and has produced hybrids, some of which are first-rate shrubs. One of the most beautiful of these is *D. elegantissima* which is shorter and broader, not exceeding 5 feet but as much as 7 feet through, with thin, arching branches wreathed in rose-pink flowers in May. This is one of the best of all deutzias.

Deutzia gracilis is more often seen as a pot plant in the greenhouse than

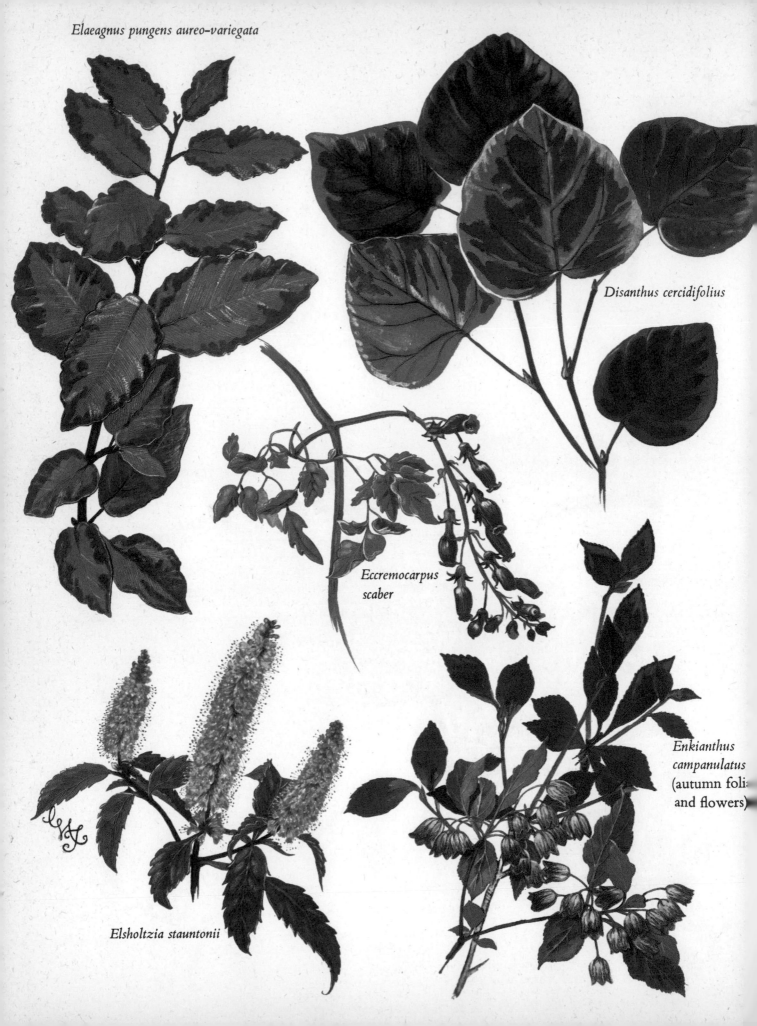

Elaeagnus pungens aureo–variegata

Disanthus cercidifolius

Eccremocarpus
scaber

Enkianthus
campanulatus
(autumn foli:
and flowers)

Elsholtzia stauntonii

Erica mediterranea

Erica arborea

rica carnea
ing George

Erica vagans Mrs D. F. Maxwell

Cynthia Newsome-Taylor

Erica darleyensis

Embothrium coccineum lanceolatum

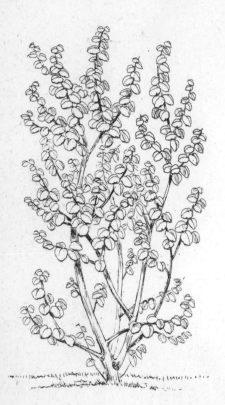

Disanthus cercidifolius

Eccremocarpus scaber

out of doors because its young growth is tender. But it can be grown successfully in the open where late spring frosts are not likely to occur. It will grow 4 feet tall and through and the pure white flowers are produced in May.

All these deutzias will grow in a wide range of soils and situations, in full sun or partial shade. The older wood is inclined to die out and, to avoid this, bushes may be pruned annually, immediately after flowering, when all the flowering stems can be cut out, leaving the young non-flowering shoots to take over.

Propagation is by cuttings of firm young growth in July or August in a propagating frame or under mist, or by larger cuttings of fully ripe growth in October or November in a sheltered position outdoors.

DIPELTA Deciduous shrubs allied to, and closely resembling, weigela. The species most commonly cultivated is *Dipelta floribunda*, a loosely branched shrub growing to 12 feet high and as much through and producing, in May, pale pink flowers with a flush of yellow in the throat. It is quite hardy and easily grown in almost any soil and open position. When flowers fade the flowering stems can be cut back as far as non-flowering shoots. Propagation is by cuttings of firm young shoots in June-July in a propagating frame or under mist, or by cuttings of fully ripe growth in October-November in a sheltered place outdoors.

DISANTHUS The only species, *Disanthus cercidifolius*, is a vigorous shrub allied to the Witch Hazel but grown primarily for its fine autumn colour. The flowers, produced in autumn, are deep purple and not attractive in either appearance or scent but the leaves, shaped like those of a Judas Tree, turn orange and crimson before they fall. The bush will grow to a height of 10 feet and 7 or 8 feet through and requires no regular pruning. It will grow in loamy or peaty soil in sun or partial shade. It can be increased by seed sown in a frame or greenhouse in spring.

DRIMYS Aromatic shrubs of which by far the best known is *Drimys winteri*. This has large shining evergreen leaves and, under very favourable conditions, will attain the proportions of a tree, but in Britain is usually seen as a big shrub up to 15 feet in height. The ivory-white flowers, which appear in May, are fragrant but it is as a foliage plant that *D. winteri* is chiefly valued. It is distinctly tender and liable to lose its young leading growths in late winter or early spring. For this reason it is really only suitable for planting in the mildest parts of the country, where it will grow in full sun or partial shade in good loamy or peaty soil. No regular pruning is required. Propagation is by cuttings of firm young growth in June-July in a propagating box or under mist with bottom heat; or by layering in spring or early summer.

ECCREMOCARPUS (Glory Flower) This climber is rather tender and often behaves like a herbaceous plant, dying down to ground level each winter but shooting up again in spring from its fleshy roots. The only species is *Eccremocarpus scaber* and it grows very quickly, soon covering quite a large screen or trellis. The tubular flowers are orange-red and very freely produced throughout the summer. The plant seeds freely and can be readily propagated by this means, for seed sown in a greenhouse in February, in a temperature of 18°C. (65°F.), will germinate quickly and the seedlings will flower the same year. *E. scaber* likes good well-drained soil and should be planted in a warm, sunny position. Some dry straw or bracken placed over the roots and base of the plant in autumn will help it to survive the winter.

ELAEAGNUS (Oleaster) Only one species is really well known in gardens, *Elaeagnus pungens*, and this almost always in one or other of its several variegated forms. It is a vigorous and hardy evergreen, making a well-branched bush up to 12 feet high and as much through. The little silvery flowers, appearing in October to November, are insignificant but fragrant and the shrub is grown mainly for its leaves, which in the variety *aureo-variegata* are bright green heavily blotched with yellow. On a sunny winter's day there are few brighter plants in the garden than this.

Elaeagnus commutata, known as the Silver Berry because of its silvery egg-shaped seed vessels, is a very different shrub, deciduous, not as a rule above 4 or 5 feet high though it can reach 12 feet, spreading so readily by underground stems that it can become invasive. It is valuable for its very silvery leaves and is often known as *E. argentea*.

Other species grown are *E. macrophylla*, an evergreen with leaves that are silvery all over when young but turn green on top as they age, and *E. angustifolia* with narrow leaves, silvery beneath, grey-green above. *E. macrophylla* is a robust shrub 12 feet high and nearly as much through. *E. angustifolia* can attain the proportions of a small tree.

All will grow in any ordinary soil and a sunny or partially shady place. They need not be pruned but, if they become too big, they can be cut back moderately in spring. All can be increased by cuttings of firm young growth in summer in a propagating frame or under mist and *E. commutata* also by digging up rooted suckers any time between October and April.

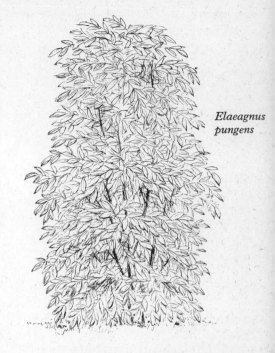

Elaeagnus pungens

ELSHOLTZIA   Half shrub, half herbaceous plant, *Elsholtzia stauntonii* is grown partly for the fragrance of its leaves which, when bruised, smell of mint, partly for its narrow spikes of purplish-pink flowers which come late in the season from August to October when flowers are scarce in the shrub border. It will reach 5 feet in a season but most of this may be cut back in winter, though given a warm, sunny place and good well-drained soil, it will shoot up again freely enough the following spring. It is increased by cuttings of firm young growth in summer in a propagating frame or under mist. The only pruning necessary is the removal of weather-damaged growth each April.

EMBOTHRIUM (Chilean Fire Bush)   In a favourable place *Embothrium coccineum* will quickly assume the proportions of a small tree, but with a little pruning, including the shortening or removal of leading shoots in June, it can be formed into a large bush, 12 to 15 feet high and 7 or 8 feet through. It has shining evergreen leaves and, in May, clusters of curled narrowly tubular scarlet flowers that are immensely decorative. The ordinary wild form is none too hardy and is really only suitable for the mildest parts of the country, but there is a variety, named *lanceolatum*, with narrower semi-evergreen leaves which is far hardier and specially free-flowering. Embothriums like well-drained lime-free soils and sunny positions. Any necessary pruning to preserve shape and restrict size should be done after flowering. They can be increased by cuttings of firm young shoots from June to August in a propagating frame or under mist with soil warming.

Enkianthus campanulatus

ENKIANTHUS   Deciduous shrubs, rather like azaleas in habit of growth, with nodding clusters of small bell-shaped flowers in May. The species most commonly planted is *Enkianthus campanulatus* which grows 5 or 6 feet high and 3 to 4 feet through. There is variation in the colour of the flowers which may be anything from soft yellow tipped with red to deep reddish-bronze. The leaves turn yellow and crimson before they fall. All kinds of enkianthus require similar conditions to azaleas, *i.e.*, peaty soils, reasonably drained but not too dry in summer, and some shade. No pruning is required. Propagation is by seed sown on sandy peat in a frame or greenhouse in spring, or by cuttings of firm young growth in June or July in sandy peat in a propagating frame or under mist.

ERICA (Heath, Heather)   From a garden standpoint the species of *Erica* may be loosely divided into two groups, the low-growing kinds and the tall or 'tree' heathers. The five most important low-growing species are *Erica carnea*, 9 to 12 inches high, flowering from February to April; *E. ciliaris*, the Dorset Heath, 9 to 12 inches high, flowering from mid-summer to autumn; *E. cinerea*, the Scotch or Bell Heather, 12 to 15 inches high, flowering from June to September; *E. tetralix*, the Cross-leaved Heath, 9 to 15 inches high, flowering from June to October; and *E. vagans*, the Cornish Heath, 12 to 18 inches high, flowering from July to October.

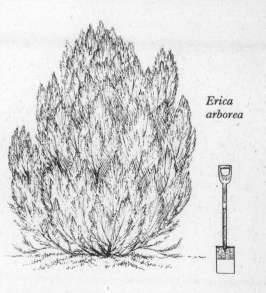

Erica arborea

Erinacea anthyllis

Eucryphia nymansensis

Eucryphia glutinosa

Escallonia langleye

Exochorda racemosa

Euonymus fortunei variegatus

Euonymus europaeus Red Cascade

Euonymus alatus

Fabiana imbricata violacea

Cynthia Newsome-Taylor

Erica vagans

Erica mediterranea

Escallonia langleyensis

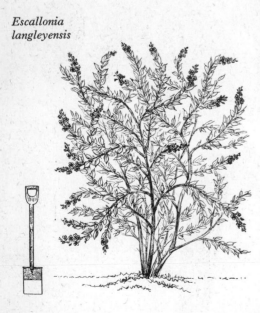

The principal tall heathers are *E. arborea*, the true Tree Heath, 8 to 10 feet high, flowering in March and April; *E. australis*, the Spanish Heath, 3 to 4 feet high, flowering in April and May; *E. lusitanica*, the Portuguese Heath, 8 to 10 feet high, flowering from February to April; *E. mediterranea*, 3 to 4 feet high, flowering from March to May; and *E. terminalis*, the Corsican Heath, 6 to 9 feet high, flowering from June to September.

In addition there is a fine hybrid between *E. carnea* and *E. mediterranea* named *E. darleyensis*. This is intermediate in height, about 1½ to 2 feet, and it flowers more or less continuously throughout the winter from November to April.

This is the bare outlines of the picture, for almost every species has its own list of varieties, often offering a range of colour from white to crimson, sometimes with double-flowered forms and coloured-leaved forms thrown in for good measure. As an example of this *E. carnea* King George is both deeper in colour and earlier in flower than *E. carnea*, and *E. vagans* Mrs. D. F. Maxwell is cerise in place of the heather pink of *E. vagans*. So varied are the heathers and so numerous that several books have been devoted entirely to them. There are nursery gardens which specialise in heathers, some growing nothing else, and there is, in Britain, a Heather Society.

Probably the very best way of growing heathers is in a heather garden, *i.e.*, a bed or series of beds devoted almost exclusively to heathers, with perhaps a few trees or shrubs for contrast. But heathers can also be brought very successfully into the general garden scheme; as ground cover so long as they are not too much in the shade, as edgings, or planted in groups towards the front of the shrub border.

All like sun and, with the exception of *E. carnea* and *E. darleyensis*, dislike lime. They thrive in open peaty, sandy or loamy soils and they benefit from being trimmed with shears or secateurs after flowering, to prevent them becoming straggly. But they should never be cut back into hard old wood which may refuse to produce new growth.

Heathers can be increased by cuttings or by layering. Cuttings are taken in summer and are prepared from firm young shoots, which may be no more than an inch in length. These are dibbled into sandy peat in a propagating frame. Layering is done in spring or early summer in a shallow trench cut out beside the plant so that some of its shoots can be bent downwards into it and be partly covered with soil, the green tips remaining uncovered. After some months the layered plants can be lifted and split up into many rooted pieces.

ERINACEA (Hedgehog Broom) A dwarf shrub with slaty-blue pea-type flowers sitting closely on a hummock of spiny growth in April and May. There is only one species, *Erinacea anthyllis*, formerly known as *E. pungens*, a shrub more suitable for the rock garden than for the shrub border. It only grows a few inches high, may eventually cover a square foot of ground and likes full sun and a well-drained soil. It can be increased from seed sown in a frame or greenhouse in spring, or by cuttings of firm young growth rooted in sand in a propagating frame in June or July.

ESCALLONIA The escallonias have a reputation for tenderness only partly deserved. Certainly some kinds, such as the very showy and popular *Escallonia macrantha*, can suffer in a cold winter and are more suitable for maritime gardens and southern or western districts than for the colder parts of Britain. But there are plenty of others that will withstand a considerable degree of frost, and as they are almost all attractive in foliage and flower some, at least, deserve to be included in most shrub planting schemes.

Escallonia rubra and *E. punctata* are both evergreen shrubs with deep red flowers throughout the late summer. They have been much used as windbreaks and for hedge making in the milder counties.

Escallonia virgata philippiana is one of the few deciduous species, a very hardy shrub, 6 to 8 feet high with arching stems and white flowers. It is seldom seen in gardens but it has bequeathed much of its hardiness and all its grace to a fine hybrid, *E. langleyensis*, which has *E. punctata* for its other parent. *E. langleyensis* is one of the best kinds for general garden planting, an evergreen shrub to 8 feet high and as much or more through, making a dense thicket of slender, arching branches wreathed with small carmine flowers around midsummer. It is typical of many other hybrids, some with larger flowers, some lighter coloured, some deeper. *E. edinensis* is much like it, Apple Blossom has pink and white flowers, C. F. Ball is crimson and Donard Seedling pale pink. There are many more, not all very distinct.

All escallonias thrive in good soil and sunny places. They are excellent seaside shrubs but will also grow well inland. No regular pruning is necessary but, if they get too big, they can be cut back in April.

Cuttings prepared from firm young stems any time from June to August root very rapidly in a propagating frame or under mist.

EUCRYPHIA Very beautiful shrubs or small trees, specially valued by connoisseurs because of their comparative rarity and the fact that they flower in July and August, a season at which the shrub garden can lack interest.

Eucryphia cordifolia is evergreen and, under favourable conditions, may reach a height of 30 feet and spread of 15 feet but is more likely to be seen at half those dimensions. The flowers are pure white with a central tuft of yellow stamens. *E. billardieri*, sometimes known as *E. lucida*, is another evergreen, of similar general character through seldom seen in gardens, probably because of its reputation for tenderness. *E. glutinosa*, which used to be known as *E. pinnatifolia* because its leaves are formed of three or five separate leaflets like those of a rose, is deciduous and will eventually grow to around 20 feet tall with a spread of 10 or 12 feet but, like *E. cordifolia*, is seldom seen above half these dimensions.

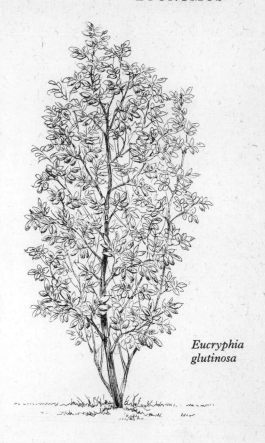

Eucryphia glutinosa

These three have produced two hybrids which are in many respects better garden plants than any of the parents. *E. nymansensis*, also known as *E. Nymansay*, is the result of crossing *E. glutinosa* and *E. cordifolia*. It is one of the tree-like kinds, growing freely to 30 feet or more with a diameter of 10 or 12 feet, making a splendid evergreen column covered with the delicate white flowers each summer. The other hybrid is known as *E. intermedia* and was produced by crossing *E. glutinosa* and *E. billardieri*. It will make a broader specimen in proportion to its height than *E. Nymansay*, perhaps 15 feet high by 10 feet broad, and the flowers are similar.

All eucryphias are a little difficult to grow. They dislike root disturbance and should be planted young, preferably from pots. They dislike lime and do best in peaty or loamy soils. All are tender to some degree, especially to late frosts and cold winds. They should be given reasonably sheltered positions where the soil immediately around them is protected by lower growing shrubs. They make excellent specimens for intermingling with rhododendrons and azaleas as they like the same soil conditions and follow them in season of flowering.

No regular pruning is required but badly placed or damaged branches can be removed in spring.

The species can be increased from seed sown in peaty soil in a frame or greenhouse in spring, but the hybrids will not come entirely true from seed and are increased either by cuttings of firm young growth in June and July, rooted under mist or, more reliably, by layering in spring or early summer.

Euonymus yedoensis

EUONYMUS (Spindle Tree) There are both evergreen and deciduous species of euonymus and they serve very different decorative needs in the garden. The evergreens, of which *Euonymus japonicus* and *E. radicans* are the most popular, are grown exclusively for their foliage which may be green or variegated. The deciduous kinds, such as *E. europaeus* and *E. latifolius*, are grown primarily for their fruits, carmine or scarlet capsules, which on ripening burst open to reveal large orange-coloured seeds. Some of these deciduous kinds also give fine autumn foliage colour.

Euonymus japonicus may eventually reach a height of 20 feet but it stands pruning so well that it is often planted as a hedge, especially near the sea as it puts up with salt spray better than most shrubs. The leaves are shining green and

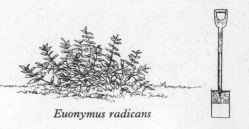

Euonymus radicans

Forsythia intermedia Lynwood

Fothergilla major

Fatsia japonica

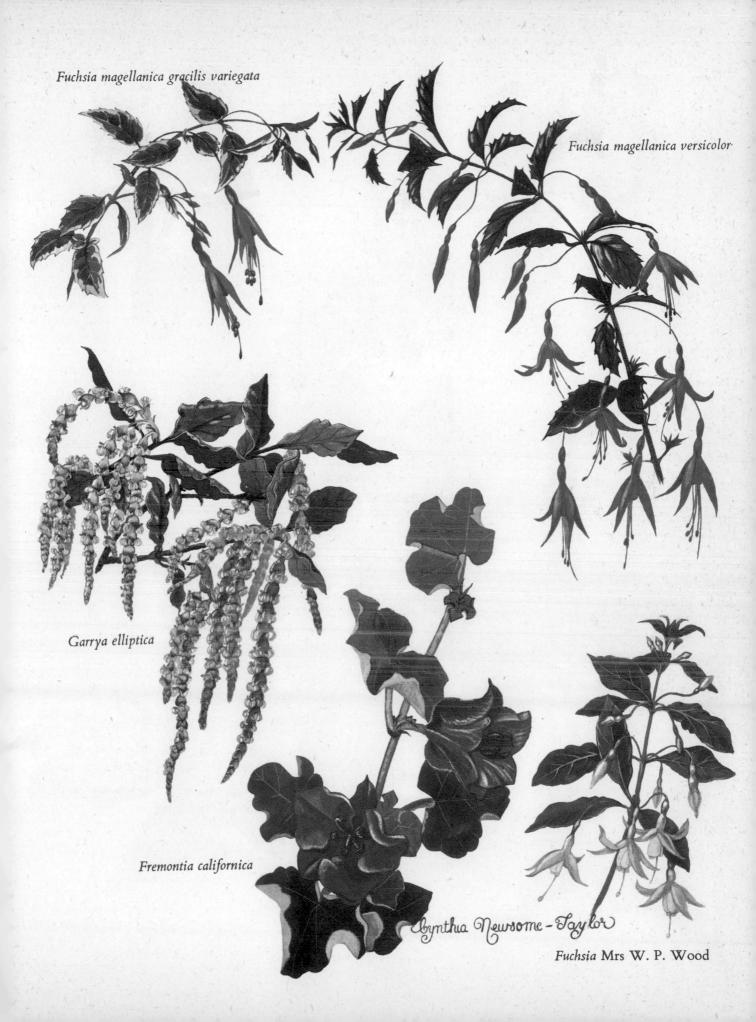

Fuchsia magellanica gracilis variegata

Fuchsia magellanica versicolor

Garrya elliptica

Fremontia californica

Cynthia Newsome-Taylor

Fuchsia Mrs W. P. Wood

Exochorda racemosa

Fabiana imbricata

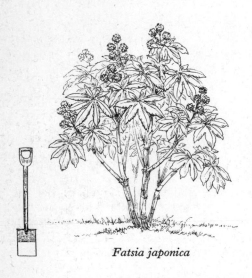

Fatsia japonica

there are several variegated forms, some with leaves blotched or edged with gold, others edged with white. One variety, named *macrophyllus*, has extra large leaves up to 3 inches long and there is a white variegated form of this. Another variety, named *microphyllus*, is dwarf and slow growing and has small leaves.

The plant which in gardens is called *E. radicans* is rather confused botanically and is probably a form of *E. fortunei*. Typically it is a creeping plant, but some forms of it make low spreading bushes. There is a form with green leaves which can be used as ground cover and, if planted against a wall or fence, will quickly ascend it. A variegated form has greyish leaves margined with white. Another green-leaved form, more bushy in habit, is known as *carrierei* and there is a variegated form of this named Silver Queen. These bushy forms will not climb or spread very far and are not so useful as ground cover.

Euonymus europaeus and *E. latifolius* both make rather loose, open bushes 6 to 10 feet high and as much through. *E. latifolius* has larger fruits and better autumn foliage colour but *E. europaeus* more than makes up in quantity of fruits what it lacks in size. Red Cascade is a particularly fine variety of *E. europaeus*. There are other species in the same general style, such as *E. yedoensis* with rose fruits and *E. sachalinensis* with scarlet fruits. Both give good autumn leaf colour, but the finest foliage effects are produced by *E. alatus*, a deciduous shrub to 8 feet high and through, with winged stems and fine pink and scarlet tints before the leaves fall.

All will grow in a great variety of soils, including chalk and light sandy soils. They will thrive in sun and the evergreen kinds will also put up with quite dense shade. The evergreens can all be pruned severely in spring or summer. As a rule the deciduous kinds need no pruning but they can be thinned or cut back in March. All are subject to attack by caterpillars and blackfly and may need to be sprayed occasionally with an insecticide.

The evergreen kinds are readily raised from cuttings in summer or autumn rooted in a frame. The creeping forms of *E. radicans* root as they spread and rooted pieces can easily be dug up in autumn or early spring. The deciduous kinds can be raised from seed sown in a frame or greenhouse in spring; from cuttings of firm young growth from June to August in a propagating frame or under mist; or they may be layered in spring or early summer.

EXOCHORDA (Pearl Bush) Deciduous shrubs of densely bushy habit with little spikes of white flowers in May. The two most commonly planted are *Exochorda giraldii* and *E. racemosa*. They are much alike, both growing 9 feet high and at least as much through. They like good, well-drained soils and open, sunny places and pay for annual pruning, immediately after flowering, when the bushes can be well thinned, some of the old flowering stems and weak shoots being removed and only the best of the younger growth retained. Propagation is by cuttings of firm young shoots in summer in a propagating frame or under mist.

FABIANA The species most commonly grown, *Fabiana imbricata*, looks rather like a tree heather, a bush 6 or 8 feet high and 4 or 5 feet through, with very small narrow leaves and, in June, plentiful but small tubular white flowers. There is a lower-growing, more spreading fabiana with mauve flowers which is sometimes called *prostrata*, sometimes *violacea*, and is variously classed as a variety of *F. imbricata* or a separate species. It has the reputation of being hardier but both need a warm sheltered position in well-drained soil. No pruning is required. Propagation is by cuttings of firm young growth in summer in a propagating frame or under mist, with soil warming.

FATSIA The only species, *Fatsia japonica*, is a handsome evergreen shrub with very large, shining green leaves, deeply lobed like those of the ivy to which it is related. But, unlike the ivy, it has no tendency to climb and makes an open, stiffly-branched shrub 8 to 10 feet high and eventually as much as 15 feet through. The flowers come in autumn and are milk-white, crowded in big branching sprays like a candelabra. It is quite surprising to find that a shrub of such luxuriant and exotic appearance is fully hardy. It likes good loamy soils and will thrive in shade, though it will also succeed in full sun. No regular pruning is required but if specimens become too large they can be reduced in size in spring. Cuttings of firm young growth will root in summer in a propagating frame with soil warming.

FORSYTHIA (Golden Bells) These are among the most popular of early-spring-flowering shrubs. All are deciduous and all have yellow flowers, though they differ in intensity of colour. *Forsythia ovata* is the first to flower, opening its primrose-coloured blooms towards the end of February and continuing into March. It makes a more compact plant than most, 5 or 6 feet high and rather more through.

Forsythia suspensa is a big, sprawling shrub with long arching branches and it can easily spread over 15 feet of ground if left to its own devices. More often it is trained to a wall or some other support and used as a climber. The flowers are sulphur-yellow and come in March or early April. It has a number of fine varieties, including *atrocaulis*, in which the stems are dark purple, *fortunei*, which is extra vigorous, and *sieboldii*, which has more slender branches.

Forsythia viridissima, the third species grown in gardens, is a much neater, more stiffly branched shrub, 6 or 7 feet high and about as much through, with bright yellow flowers in April.

But as garden plants all these species have been surpassed by a hybrid between two of them, *F. suspensa* and *F. viridissima*. This is named *F. intermedia* because it is intermediate between its parents in many ways and combines the best features of each. It has the sturdy branches and rich colour of *F. viridissima*, the vigour of *F. suspensa* and it flowers in March. Like many hybrids, it has proved variable and the best forms of it have been selected and given distinctive names such as *spectabilis* and Lynwood. These have extra large, deep yellow flowers.

All forsythias like good rich soil though they will survive almost anywhere. But to see them at their best they should be fed a little with manure or fertiliser and pruned annually after flowering, when many of the stems that are carrying faded flowers can be cut out but all the strong shoots and unflowered stems retained. The best flowers are produced on sturdy year-old stems.

Forsythias can be readily increased either by summer cuttings of firm young growth in a propagating frame or under mist, or by cuttings of fully ripe growth in October to November in a sheltered place outdoors.

FOTHERGILLA Deciduous shrubs grown primarily for their brilliant autumn foliage colour though they are also quite decorative in spring when carrying their numerous little feathery tufts of creamy fragrant flowers. The leaves are shaped like those of a hazel and change to yellow, orange or crimson before they fall. *Fothergilla gardenii*, also sometimes known as either *F. alnifolia* or *F. carolina*, grows 2 or 3 feet high and through and is the least satisfactory as it can be weak and slow growing. *F. monticola* is the species most commonly planted, a well-formed bush 5 to 7 feet high and about as much through. *F. major* is much like it, a little taller without being any broader. It can reach 10 feet under favourable conditions.

Advice on the cultivation of fothergillas is remarkable for its contradictions. One authority recommends moist soils, another light and open soils, a third suggests a combination of peat and sand. Plants have grown fairly well with me in a moist loamy soil, but the best I have seen were in a much warmer and better drained position. All can be increased by layering in spring or early summer and by cuttings of firm young growth in June to July under mist and soil warming.

FREMONTIA There are two species, *Fremontia californica* and *F. mexicana*, but from a garden standpoint they are so similar that they may be treated as one. They should be evergreen but usually find the British climate so unpleasant that they lose most of their leaves in winter. In the open they would make loosely

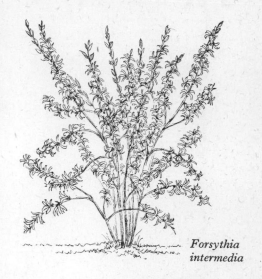

Forsythia intermedia

Fothergilla major

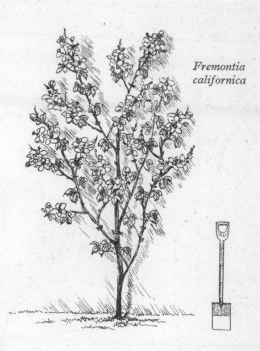

Fremontia californica

Genista virgata

Genista lydia

Genista
aethnensis

Genista hispanica

Gaultheria shallon

Grevillea rosmarinifolia

Halimium lasianthum

Hamamelis mollis

Hamamelis japonica
zuccariniana

Cynthia Newsome-Taylor

Fuchsia magellanica gracilis

Fuchsia Mrs W. P. Wood

*Garrya
elliptica*

branched shrubs, but they are more usually planted against sunny walls and trained roughly in the form of a fan. The leaves are leathery and unusual in colour, a kind of olive above and tawny beneath. They have a spicy odour when bruised. The flowers are saucer shaped, deep golden-yellow and continuously produced from May to July.

Fremontias should be given the warmest, most sheltered positions available in well-drained soil. No pruning is likely to be necessary except the removal of weather-damaged growth in spring. They can be increased by seed sown in a warm greenhouse in spring but, as fremontias transplant badly, it is desirable to pot the seedlings singly as early as possible and plant out from these pots with as little root disturbance as possible.

FUCHSIA   This is a genus which has been greatly developed in gardens and many of the large flowered kinds have been bred for greenhouse display rather than for planting permanently outdoors. There are, however, a few of a tougher, hardier character that can be grown quite successfully in the open, especially near the coast and in the South and West, where winters are less severe. There is also one species, *F. magellanica*, which is sufficiently hardy to be grown outdoors and which has numerous varieties that are equally hardy. *F. magellanica* has flowers more slenderly formed than those of the big hybrid fuchsias and this characteristic is pleasantly exaggerated in variety *gracilis* which has slender stems and long, narrow flowers with pointed segments. It is a very attractive shrub and one of the most reliable hardy fuchsias for the garden. There is also a form of it, named *variegata*, with leaves variegated with silver and pink, one of the best of all the hardy fuchsias. Very similar to this is *F. magellanica versicolor*, the leaves of which are grey-green more or less marked with cream and pink. Even stems on the same plant can vary in their colouring. Yet another variety of *F. magellanica*, named *alba*, has very pale pink flowers, not white as one might suppose. Variety *riccartonii* has small neat scarlet and purple flowers and is much used as a hedge-plant in the South-west. Varieties *pumila* and *globosa* are dwarfs.

Among the hybrid fuchsias suitable for outdoor planting are Brilliant, scarlet and purple; Display, carmine and pink; Chillerton Beauty, pink and violet; Corallina, scarlet; Madame Cornelissen, carmine and white; Margaret, carmine and purple; Mrs Popple, scarlet and purple; Tom Thumb, a dwarf with carmine and violet flowers; and Mrs W. P. Wood, soft pink.

Fuchsias are not fussy about soil but are unlikely to survive waterlogging, especially in winter. They like warm sunny places and should be planted so that the crowns (the point where stems join roots) are an inch or so below soil level. Then, in autumn, sand, old boiler ashes or peat can be placed over the crowns as further protection from frost. In a hard winter, all growth may be killed to ground level, in which case it should be cut off in March. New shoots should appear from below ground level and these will grow quickly and produce flowers from July or early August to October or even later if the autumn is mild.

All fuchsias are very easily increased by cuttings of young shoots at almost any time from spring to early autumn. The cuttings will root quickly in a propagating frame or under mist.

GARRYA   A splendid evergreen producing, in winter, long slender grey-green catkins. There are several species but only one, *Garrya elliptica*, is planted to any extent in British gardens. In the open this will make a well-branched bush, 8 to 10 feet high and as much in diameter, but it can also be trained against a wall where it can easily attain a height of 12 to 15 feet. Male and female flowers are produced on separate plants and it is the male form which should be planted for the catkin display as the catkins are much longer and more decorative than those of the female. Nevertheless the female plant is also worth growing because, if there is a male plant nearby, its shorter catkins will be followed by trails of quite handsome black fruits.

Garryas thrive in warm, sunny, sheltered places and well-drained soils. They transplant badly and are best grown in pots when young so that they can be planted with a minimum of root disturbance. They are a little tender, especially to late spring frost when young, and may need some protection for the first year or so. No regular pruning is essential but when trained against walls they can be thinned and kept in shape by pruning in April or May, after the catkins have fallen.

Propagation is by cuttings of firm young growth in July or August in a propagating frame or under mist.

GAULTHERIA Evergreen shrubs chiefly of value as ground cover. Many of them are prostrate or low-growing shrubs, but *Gaultheria shallon* may grow to 6 feet under some conditions though more commonly it is seen as a thicket-forming shrub, 2 to 3 feet in height and spreading almost indefinitely by means of suckers. It has its use as rough cover under trees as it will survive a considerable degree of shade. It has small blush-white flowers in May and June followed by deep purple berries.

A choicer plant is *G. procumbens,* a carpet-forming shrub with small dark shining green leaves and, in autumn, red berries. *G. miqueliana* is another low-growing shrub, about 9 inches high, wide-spreading with clusters of small white flowers in June followed by white berries.

All gaultherias like lime-free soils. They will thrive in cool peaty soils or soils rich in leafmould, in woodlands under similar conditions to rhododendrons and azaleas, to which they are allied. No pruning is required.

They can be increased from seed sown in sandy peat in a frame or greenhouse in spring. *G. shallon* can also be increased by suckers dug up in autumn or early spring with roots and most of the other kinds by cuttings of firm young shoots in a propagating frame or under mist in summer.

GENISTA (Broom) This is the other family of brooms, differing from *Cytisus* in botanical details concerned with the seeds. The confusion, from a garden standpoint, is increased by the fact that the one shrub which all gardeners call 'genista', freely sold as a pot plant in florists' shops, does not really belong to this genus at all but to *Cytisus.*

Nearly all genistas, and certainly all those commonly grown in gardens, have yellow flowers but they differ enormously in height and habit. One of the largest is *Genista aethnensis*, a shrub so tall that it might almost be regarded as a small tree. It will reach 12 feet quite easily and may on occasion attain 20 feet. It is usually narrower than it is tall and it has thin weeping branches wreathed, in July, with small yellow flowers. It is an exceptionally graceful plant, admirable as an isolated specimen or at the back of the shrub border, but because of its height and the rather light anchorage, typical of most brooms, it needs secure staking.

Genista cinerea is another big shrub, 8 to 10 feet high and fully as much through, with sweet-scented golden-yellow flowers in June and July. It closely resembles *G. virgata*, a species often known as the Madeira Broom because that is where it grows wild. Despite this very mild habitat, *G. virgata* is quite hardy in Britain.

Very different in habit and style is the Spanish Gorse, *G. hispanica*. This does look rather like a neat fine-leaved gorse bush, no more than 2 feet high but in time spreading to a diameter of 5 or 6 feet. It is spiny like gorse and has small gorse-like flowers very freely produced in May and early June.

Genista lydia is a little beauty, 2 to 3 feet high but spreading to 5 or 6 feet, with arching stems thickly covered with yellow flowers in June. It looks well on a dry wall or in a rock garden. These are also good places for *G. tinctoria*, the Dyer's Greenweed, which only rises to about 9 inches but spreads its thin shoots out in all directions to cover a diameter of 6 feet or more in time. The most decorative form, known as *plena*, has double yellow flowers. Like the single-flowered kind, it flowers in June. *G. sagittalis* is yet another prostrate kind, but not quite so wide spreading as *G. tinctoria*. It has winged stems and yellow flowers in June and is equally suitable for dry wall or rock garden.

All genistas like light well-drained soils. Like cytisus they can be lightly

Genista aethnensis

Genista virgata

Genista hispanica

Hedysarum multijugum

Hebe andersonii variegata

Hebe Great Orme

Hebe Midsummer Beauty

Hedera helix conglomerata

Hibiscus syriacus
Blue Bird

Hibiscus syriacus
Hamabo

Hibiscus syriacus
Woodbridge

*Hedera colchica
variegata*

*Hedera helix
sagittaefolia*

Cynthia Newsome-Taylor

Genista lydia

Grevillea rosmarinifolia

Halimium ocymoides

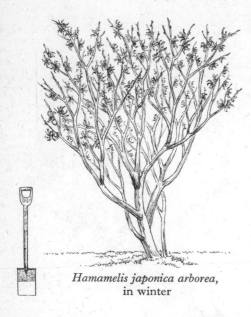

Hamamelis japonica arborea,
in winter

pruned after flowering to keep them neat and prevent them spreading too far, but they should not be cut back into old hard wood which may refuse to produce new growth. All are sun lovers.

All can be increased from seed and also from cuttings of firm young shoots inserted in June or July in a propagating frame or under mist.

GREVILLEA Evergreen shrubs all of which are, to some extent, tender. *Grevillea sulphurea* has the reputation of being the hardiest but even this must be planted in sheltered places, except in the mildest parts of the country. It will grow 3 or 4 feet high and as much through, has narrow leaves like those of a rosemary and curiously formed, light yellow flowers all the summer. The resemblance to rosemary is emphasised in the name of *G. rosmarinifolia*, a shrub of rather similar appearance to the last, but with crimson flowers. Both kinds should be planted in the warmest, sunniest, most sheltered position available. They thrive in peaty or light loamy soils and do not like chalk. They can be increased by cuttings in summer of firm young growths in a propagating frame or under mist with soil warming.

HALIMIUM These sun-loving evergreens are closely allied to both *Helianthemum* and *Cistus* and have all been included at some time in one or other of those two genera. Now, on botanical grounds, they have been given separate status but from a garden standpoint they may be considered as an extension of the genus *Helianthemum*, to be given similar treatment and to be propagated in the same way.

Halimium halimifolium is a neat little bush, 2 to 3 feet high and barely as much through, with yellow maroon-spotted flowers in May and June. *H. lasianthum* may appear in gardens as *Helianthemum formosum*. It is 2 to 3 feet high and can cover 5 or 6 feet of ground with its grey-downy shoots and leaves. The flowers come in May and June and are yellow blotched with purple.

Halimium libanotis also passes as *Helianthemum rosmarinifolium*. It is much like another species, *H. umbellatum*, for both have neat rosemary-like leaves and grow about 18 inches high and as much through. But whereas *H. libanotis* has yellow flowers those of *H. umbellatum* are white.

One of the best known kinds is *H. ocymoides*. This was once called *Helianthemum algarvense* and this name lingers on in gardens and nurseries. This species grows 3 feet high and 4 or 5 feet through, with grey leaves and very bright yellow flowers with an almost black blotch at the base of each petal.

All are shrubs for warm sunny places and well-drained soils. They can be damaged by severe frosts and may be in particular need of some protection the first winter after planting. They can be raised from seed sown in a frame or greenhouse in spring, or by summer cuttings of firm young growth in a propagating frame or under mist.

HAMAMELIS (Witch Hazel) The witch hazels have the merit of flowering in mid-winter and of being completely hardy, but they suffer the drawback of being rather large for the ordinary shrub border. One at least, *Hamamelis japonica*, will grow to the proportions of a small tree and has an extra vigorous variety which is actually known as *arborea*. There are several colour forms of this, the typical *H. japonica* having yellow flowers, *arborea* yellow and purple flowers, *flavo-purpurascens* or *rubra* orange and purple flowers and *zuccariniana* lemon flowers. All flower in January and February.

The most popular, on account of the size of its flowers, is *H. mollis*. This will easily reach 15 feet, making a big spreading shuttlecock bush fully as broad as it is tall. Typically its flowers are rich yellow but there is a variety, named *pallida*, which has pale yellow flowers. All forms are fragrant and the flowers come in December and January. The earliest species to bloom, in October and November, is *H. virginiana* which is also yellow.

All like good rich, loamy soils not liable to dry out in summer. Pruning is not essential but badly placed or overgrown branches can be removed or shortened in February or March as soon as the flowers have faded. All can be raised from

GENISTA

64

seed sown in a frame or greenhouse but this usually takes two years to germinate and then several more years must elapse before the seedlings attain flowering size. A further drawback is that the varieties may not come true to colour from seed. For all these reasons, nurserymen usually graft on to seedlings of *H. virginiana*, doing this in spring in a greenhouse. For amateurs a more practical method of increasing is by layering in spring or early summer.

HEBE Evergreen shrubs which were formerly known as *Veronica* and will still be found under that name in many gardens and nurseries. Many are valuable garden plants because of their long flowering season but several of the most decorative are on the border-line of hardiness. This is true of all the large-flowered hybrids of *Hebe speciosa*, plants which have received garden names such as Gloriosa, pink; La Seduisante, crimson; Alicia Amherst, violet; and Simon Delaux, deep crimson. These are all first-class seaside shrubs, flowering more or less continuously from July to October. All have fairly broad shining green leaves and make well-branched shrubs 3 to 4 feet high and rather more through.

Rather hardier than these are *H. salicifolia* and its hybrids. Typical *H. salicifolia* has narrow leaves and long slender spikes of white flowers and grows up to 10 feet high and at least as much through. But there are a great many forms and hybrids and it is difficult to tell where *H. salicifolia* stops and some other species takes over. Midsummer Beauty is one of the best garden varieties in this group, a shrub 3 to 4 feet high and 5 or 6 feet through with spikes of lavender flowers from July to November or even later if the weather permits. It is a little tender. *H. andersonii* also belongs here, probably with *H. speciosa* as its other parent, a shrub with violet and white flowers most useful in a form which has leaves variegated with creamy-white. The parentage of other hybrids, such as pink-flowered Great Orme and violet Mrs E. Tennant, is more difficult to place with any certainty so readily do hebes cross.

One of the hardiest species is *H. brachysiphon*, still known in most gardens as *Veronica traversii*. This makes a big rounded bush, 5 or 6 feet high and 6 or 8 feet through, with neat box-like foliage and short spikes of white flowers in July.

Hebe hulkeana is one of the more tender kinds and usually requires the protection of a south- or west-facing wall. It grows 3 to 4 feet tall, occasionally more, and has big sprays of lavender flowers in May and June.

There are smaller species, such as *H. macrantha* with quite large, white flowers in May. This makes a bush to about 2 feet high and through, occasionally more. *H. carnosula* makes a broad, dome-shaped bush 2 feet high and 4 or 5 feet across. Its white flowers appear in June and July. *H. pagei* is no more than a foot high but as much as 3 feet across, and has white flowers in June and July. Then there is *H. cupressoides*, a 1 to 2 foot bush with leaves so small and closely held to the stems that it might be mistaken for a conifer. *H. hectori* and *H. pinguifolia* are others of the same type.

All hebes will grow in a wide range of soils and are not in the least fussy in this respect. They like warm sunny places and the more tender kinds should only be planted in the milder parts of the country, unless winter protection can be given. No regular pruning is necessary but if bushes become too big they can be thinned and reduced in the spring.

All are very easily increased by cuttings of firm young shoots taken at any time from May to October and inserted in sandy soil in a frame. Seed will germinate readily and self-sown seedlings may appear quite freely in favourable places. As some of these hebes hybridise readily, seedlings may show considerable variation from their parents and can be most interesting.

HEDERA (Ivy) The ivies have acquired an almost entirely unjustified reputation for causing damage to trees and buildings. Only on old houses built with lime mortar or on old and decayed trees are they really dangerous. Vigorous trees can easily outgrow them and walls bonded with cement are unaffected by them. The best varieties are very decorative and some of the smaller leaved and less vigorous varieties make excellent ground cover. Though all ivies climb by

Hebe salicifolia

Hebe cupressoides

Hedera colchica dentata variegata

Hydrangea paniculata grandiflora

Hydrangea serrata

Hydrangea macrophylla Hamburg

Hydrangea villosa

Hydrangea petiolaris

Hydrangea serrata
Grayswood

Hydrangea macrophylla
Générale Vicomtesse de Vibraye

Cynthia Newsome-Taylor

Hedera helix conglomerata

Hedysarum multijugum

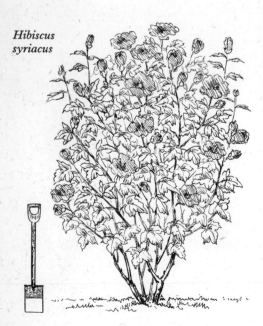

Hibiscus syriacus

means of aerial rootlets, when they flower and fruit they do so on bushy non-climbing stems with leaves that are without lobes and, if cuttings are rooted from these, they will retain the bushy non-climbing habit and can be used like shrubs.

The English ivy is *Hedera helix* and in its common form is so widespread that it is hardly worth introducing to gardens. But it has many varieties, some of great interest and beauty. These differ in the vigour of their growth and the shape and colour of their leaves. The name given to the bushy, flowering non-climbing form referred to above is *arborescens* and there are varieties of this with silver or golden variegated leaves. The varieties *conglomerata* and *congesta* are very dense slow-growing climbers that will take years to reach 2 or 3 feet. They can be planted quite safely in the rock garden. The variety *sagittaefolia* has small arrow-shaped leaves and *caenwoodiana* has deeply cut finger-like lobes to the leaves. In *deltoidea* the leaves are big and triangular and the two basal lobes overlap, and *tortuosa* has leaves that are curled or twisted. Variety *aureo-variegata* has green leaves suffused with yellow and *discolor* has leaves splashed with cream and red. In *marginata major* the leaves are edged with silver and in Jubilee Gold Heart there is a blotch of gold in the centre of each small dark green leaf. The variety *purpurea* has green leaves in summer, but they become bronze-purple in winter. So one might go on, for whole books have been written about the varieties of ivy.

There are several other species besides English ivy. Most useful in the garden is *H. colchica*, an ivy with very large, almost un-lobed leaves. It has a beautiful variety, heavily variegated with pale yellow, which is known either as *variegata* or as *dentata variegata*.

Hedera canariensis, the Canary Island Ivy, is rather tender and usually grown as a house plant, but it can be established outdoors in mild places. It has large leaves which are without lobes or only shallowly lobed, and there is a good variegated variety in which the leaves are edged with cream.

All these ivies can be grown in any soil, in sun or shade. They can be trimmed over or cut back in spring if they get untidy or grow too big. Planted against a low fence and trimmed two or three times each year, they can be used instead of a hedge. Such a method of training is sometimes referred to as a 'fedge', *i.e.* a combination of fence and hedge.

Ivies are very easily layered at any time of year, and cuttings prepared from the younger shoots will also root readily in a frame in summer or autumn.

HEDYSARUM Deciduous shrubs of loose open habit with small pea-like flowers freely produced over a long season. One of the best is *Hedysarum multijugum*, with purple flowers more or less all the summer. It grows 4 to 5 feet high and rather more through and makes long arching branches with small compound leaves, giving a very graceful appearance. It will thrive in any ordinary soil but prefers light well-drained soils and sunny situations. No regular pruning is required but overgrown bushes can be thinned or reduced in March. Propagation is by seed sown in greenhouse or frame in spring or by cuttings of firm young growth in summer in a propagating frame or under mist.

HIBISCUS Many species of hibiscus are only suitable for cultivation in warm climates or greenhouses but one, *Hibiscus syriacus*, is quite hardy. It is a rather stiffly branched shrub 8 or 9 feet high and 7 or 8 feet through with flowers like small single hollyhocks produced in August and September. The flowers may be white or various shades of blue, purple, pink, rose or crimson and may also be either single or double. Numbers of these varieties have been named. Woodbridge is a fine deep rose-pink single, Blue Bird is single and deep blue, Hamabo is single and blush with crimson blotches, Duc de Brabant is double and red, Souvenir de Charles Breton is double and lilac and many more will be found in nursery catalogues. In addition another species is now available named *H. sinosyriacus*. It is similar in general appearance and habit but has larger leaves.

All like good well-drained soils and sunny situations. They often transplant badly and may make little or no growth the first year, but when established they grow fairly fast. Pruning is not essential but overgrown plants can be thinned or reduced in April. Propagation is by layering in spring or early summer or by cuttings of firm young growth in summer in a propagating frame or under mist.

HYDRANGEA This is one of the big genera of deciduous shrubs, of great importance in the garden because of the number of highly decorative varieties that have been produced and the fact that these flower in summer, after the main flowering season of shrubs.

By far the most popular are the numerous varieties of *Hydrangea macrophylla*, a big well-branched shrub of rounded habit which will soon reach a height of 6 or 8 feet and a still greater girth. For convenience the garden varieties of this hydrangea are usually split up into two groups, one often known as the Lacecaps because of the form of their flower heads which are flat and made up of a number of small fertile flowers surrounded by a ring of much larger infertile flowers, and the other, known as the Hortensias, with large almost globular flower heads entirely formed of the showy infertile flowers.

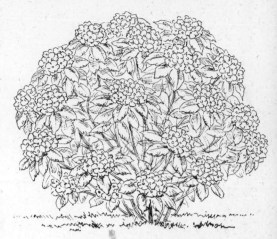

Hydrangea macrophylla hortensia

Colours range from white and pale mauve or pink to quite deep blue, purple, rose or crimson. There is, however, an odd thing about hydrangea colours. They change according to the nature of the soil. If this is acid they tend to be more blue or if alkaline they become more pink or red. It is quite possible to get flowers of different colours on plants of the same variety growing in different parts of the garden and even, sometimes, in flowers on the same plant. Only the white varieties, being devoid of pigment, remain unchanged whatever soil they are in. It is possible to modify or change the colour by treating the soil around the bushes, either with lime to make them more red or with alum to make them more blue. But these treatments are more effective and practical when hydrangeas are grown in pots or tubs than when they are planted in the open ground. Générale Vicomtesse de Vibraye is one of the best blue varieties, Hamburg a good deep pink.

Closely allied to *H. macrophylla* and much like its Lacecap varieties in appearance is *H. serrata*. It does not make so much growth and bushes rarely exceed 3 feet in height and diameter. Colours are white, pink or light blue. Grayswood is a typical variety.

Hydrangea paniculata grandiflora

There are many other hydrangeas worth growing. One of the best, *H. paniculata*, has more cone-shaped heads of creamy-white flowers. These come in July and August and may be of medium size and very freely produced in the form known as *floribunda* or be less numerous but individually larger in the form known as *grandiflora*. Either will grow 6 to 8 feet high and as much through. Another species with creamy flowers, but in a rounded instead of a cone-shaped head, is *H. arborescens*. It will grow 4 to 5 feet high and 5 to 6 feet through and it flowers in July and August. So does *H. quercifolia*, a bush of similar size and habit, also with creamy flower heads, but with leaves shaped like those of an oak, though much larger.

Hydrangea villosa is a very beautiful species, with Lacecap flower heads in two shades of purplish-blue. It makes a big broad bush 7 to 9 feet high and as much as 12 feet through in old specimens. *H. sargentiana* has larger heads of similar colour but the habit is quite different, tall but rather gaunt. Plants may reach 6 or 8 feet but be only half that through. It appreciates shelter.

There is even a climbing hydrangea, *H. petiolaris*, which clings by aerial roots, like an ivy, and has flat heads of white flowers in June.

Hydrangea villosa

All these hydrangeas thrive in good rich soils. Many of them will grow in full sun but some, such as *H. serrata* and *H. sargentiana*, prefer partial shade and all can be grown well in thin woodland. Many are a little tender, particularly to spring frosts which may kill the expanding buds, check growth and prevent flowering. These troubles are most apparent in young plants and those growing in full exposure, but hydrangeas should not be planted in places where severe spring frosts are common.

Some kinds need no pruning but *H. paniculata* can be cut back quite hard each April, treatment which reduces the size of the bush but increases the size

Indigofera gerardiana

Hypericum patulum Hidcote

Kalmia latifolia

Jasminum humile revolutum

Hypericum moserianum

Lavandula spica

Lavatera olbia rosea

Kolkwitzia amabilis

Lavandula spica
Hidcote

Kerria japonica pleniflora

Cynthia Newsome-Taylor

Hydrangea petiolaris

Hypericum moserianum

Hypericum patulum Hidcote

Indigofera gerardiana

of the flower heads. *H. macrophylla* and its varieties can be thinned a little in spring and the faded flower heads should then be removed, but care should be taken not to remove the sturdy buds towards the tops of strong stems as it is from these that the flowers will be produced.

All hydrangeas can be increased by cuttings of firm young growth taken at practically any time in spring and summer and rooted in a frame or under mist. Cuttings root quickly and, if potted singly as soon as rooted and grown on in a frame, many kinds will commence to flower the following year.

HYPERICUM (St John's Wort, Rose of Sharon)   These are valuable shrubs because of the ease with which they can be grown and their long flowering season. All have yellow flowers. *Hypericum calycinum*, the Rose of Sharon, is a sprawling evergreen that will not exceed 18 inches in height but will continue to spread indefinitely by stems which root as they go. The flowers, which come from June to August, are large and each has a conspicuous central tuft of golden stamens which adds to their beauty. This is a splendid shrub for covering banks and rough places but it can become invasive and smother smaller plants.

More moderate in growth is *H. moserianum*, a hybrid between *H. calycinum* and *H. patulum*. This grows about 2 feet high and is unlikely to exceed 3 feet in spread. It has saucer-shaped flowers in July and August and is deciduous. *H. patulum* itself is in many ways the most useful species of all for gardens. Typically a densely branched deciduous bush, 3 to 4 feet high and a little more through with saucer-shaped golden-yellow flowers throughout the summer, it has produced several excellent varieties with even better qualities. Varieties *henryi* and *forrestii* have larger, better formed flowers and Hidcote has even bigger flowers, makes a bush up to 6 feet high and if the winter is not too severe, is more or less evergreen.

All these hypericums will thrive in a great variety of soils. *H. calycinum* will put up with quite dense shade and can be planted under shrubs and in woodlands as well as in full sun. The others prefer sunny positions. No regular pruning is required.

All can be increased by summer cuttings of firm young growth in a propagating frame or under mist. *H. calycinum* can also be increased by division any time between October and April. Hypericums can also be raised from seed sown in a frame or greenhouse in the spring but there may be some variation in flower size and form.

INDIGOFERA (Indigo)   Deciduous shrubs of open, arching habit, with graceful rather ferny leaves and little spikes of pea-type flowers produced continuously in late summer and early autumn. One of the best is *Indigofera gerardiana*, which grows 3 to 4 feet tall and may be as much as 8 feet through. The flowers are rosy-purple and come from July to September. *I. hebepetala* grows more slowly but may eventually reach 6 feet. Its purplish-pink and crimson flowers are produced, later than most, in August and September. *I. potaninii* will reach 8 feet and has rather long spikes of lilac-pink flowers.

All like good well-drained soils and sunny sheltered positions. They are liable to frost damage in winter, especially when young, but will usually throw up strong new growth from the base. Any damaged growth can be cut out in April and, at the same time, overgrown plants can be thinned. Indigoferas can be raised from seed sown in a greenhouse in spring, or by cuttings of firm young growth in summer in a propagating frame or under mist.

JASMINUM (Jasmine, Jessamine)   The common jasmine, *Jasminum officinale*, is a climber and the winter jasmine, *J. nudiflorum*, is also usually grown as a climber though strictly it is a shrub of loose and sprawling habit. But by no means all jasmines are climbers and at least one, *J. humile revolutum*, makes an excellent bush 5 feet high and as much through. *J. officinale* is deciduous, vigorous and will cover quite a large fence or trellis with its thin twining stems. The white flowers, which appear in July and August, are very fragrant. *J. nudiflorum* is also deciduous and will reach 10 feet against a wall but left to its own devices in the open would not exceed 6 feet, though it might be easily twice that in breadth. The bright yellow flowers come from November to February and have no fragrance. *J. humile revolutum* is evergreen and produces its yellow moderately fragrant flowers in June and July. *J. primulinum* is not unlike *J. nudiflorum* but is evergreen and has larger flowers produced from April to June.

All the jasmines will grow in a great variety of soils. Most like sunny positions, but *J. nudiflorum* will succeed very well trained against a north-facing wall. *J. humile revolutum* is liable to be damaged by frost in winter, so should have a reasonably sheltered position. This is also essential for *J. primulinum* which is really only suitable for the mildest places.

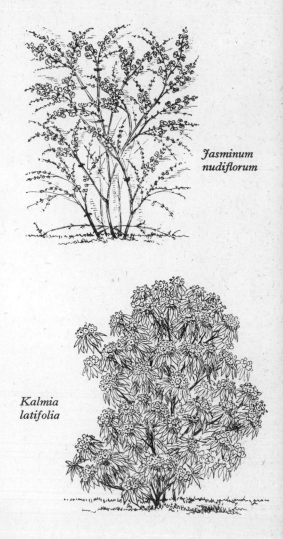

Jasminum nudiflorum

If it becomes overgrown *J. officinale* can be thinned and shortened in March. *J. nudiflorum* can be thinned and shortened after flowering to keep it in bounds. If *J. humile revolutum* is damaged by frost, these stems can be cut out in April, at which time overgrown bushes can also be thinned.

Jasmines can be increased by layering in spring or early summer and also by summer cuttings of firm young growth in summer in a propagating frame or under mist.

KALMIA (Calico Bush, Sheep Laurel) Beautiful evergreen shrubs for lime-free soils. The most popular is *Kalmia latifolia*, the Calico Bush, a bush very much like a rhododendron in habit, 8 to 10 feet high and as much or slightly more through, with abundant clusters of bright pink flowers in June. Individually the flowers look rather like small Chinese lanterns and this is one of the most beautiful of all early-summer-flowering evergreens.

Kalmia angustifolia, the Sheep Laurel, is not above 3 feet in height and often considerably less, spreading slowly but indefinitely by means of suckers and bearing crowded clusters of rosy-red flowers in June. *K. glauca* is small but bushy, 1 to 2 feet high and as much in diameter and carries its pale rosy-purple flowers in April.

All require conditions similar to rhododendrons and are very suitable for associating with them. They like peaty, humus-rich soils not liable to dry out in summer but not waterlogged in winter. No pruning is required.

All can be increased by seed sown in sandy peat in a frame or greenhouse in spring, or by cuttings of firm young growth in July or August in a propagating frame or under mist.

Kalmia latifolia

KERRIA There is only one species, *Kerria japonica*, but it has two forms which differ considerably in growth and consequently in the use to which they can be put in the garden. The wild form has single yellow flowers, freely produced in April and May, and it makes a thicket of growth, usually about 5 feet high but quite often considerably more through as it goes on spreading by offsets almost like a herbaceous plant. The other form, known as *pleniflora* and popularly as Batchelors Buttons, has fully double flowers like golden pompons. It also differs in habit, being considerably taller but not so inclined to spread. Its stems, less twiggy and stouter than those of the wild form but still pliable, can reach a length of 10 or 12 feet and for this reason this kerria is frequently treated as a climber, being trained against walls or on fences or screens.

Kerria japonica pleniflora

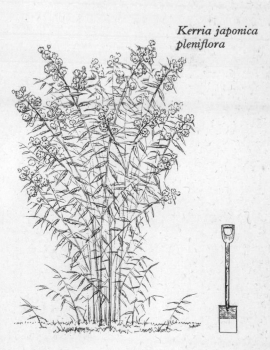

Both forms are very easy to grow in almost any soil. They will thrive in full sun or partial shade and can be thinned or shortened after flowering.

It is often possible to increase them by division or by digging out rooted pieces, any time between October and April. The younger stems can be layered in spring or early summer, or cuttings of firm young growth can be rooted in June or July in a propagating frame or under mist, preferably with soil warming.

KOLKWITZIA In America *Kolkwitzia amabilis* is called Beauty Bush, a not inappropriate name as a good form of this deciduous shrub is a very beautiful sight when in flower in May and June. It looks much like a very graceful weigela, more freely branched and with thinner stems bearing compound leaves which add to the effect. The flowers are soft pink with a touch of yellow in the throat

Leycesteria formosa (fruit)

*Ligustrum ovalifolium
aureo-marginatum*

*Leycesteria
formosa*
(flowers)

*Leptospermum
scoparium
nichollsii*

Leucothoë catesbaei

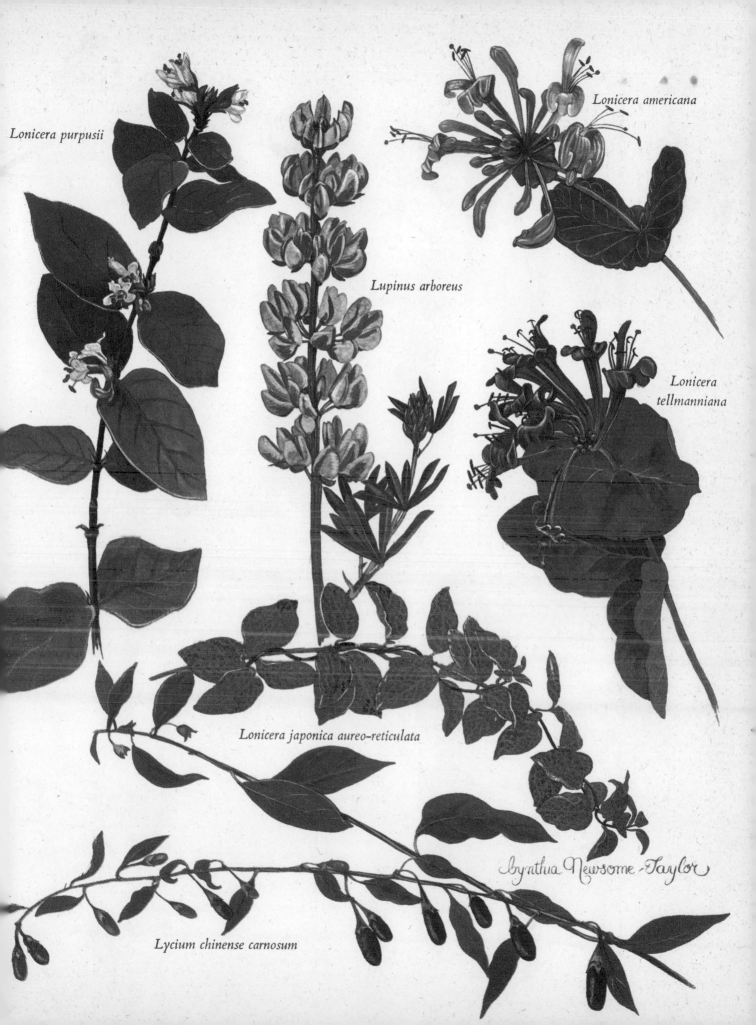

Lonicera purpusii

Lonicera americana

Lupinus arboreus

Lonicera tellmanniana

Lonicera japonica aureo-reticulata

Lycium chinense carnosum

Cynthia Newsome-Taylor

Kolkwitzia amabilis

Lavandula spica

Lavandula Hidcote

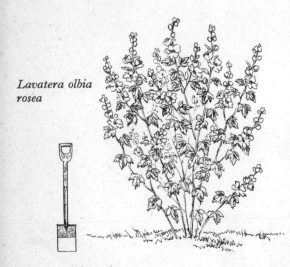

Lavatera olbia rosea

and are produced with immense freedom in good forms, though there are some inferior forms which flower sparsely. A bush will reach 6 to 8 feet in height and as much or a little more through. *K. amabilis* is not fussy about soil, likes a sunny place and is all the better for a little thinning after flowering, when stems bearing faded flowers can be removed to make room for the younger growth. Propagation is by cuttings of firm young growth in July or August in a propagating frame or under mist.

LAVANDULA (Lavender) It is strange that a shrub so well known as the lavender and so long cultivated in gardens should have a confused nomenclature, but so it is. Perhaps it is just because it has been grown for hundreds of years and has a natural tendency to vary in height, breadth of leaf, length of flower spike and flower colour that muddles have arisen. Certain it is that names proliferate in books and catalogues and that it is often difficult to determine whether they really do represent distinct varieties or are synonyms. Even the precise status of the species from which these garden forms have arisen seems to be in doubt. Most catalogues list two separate 'common' species of lavender: *Lavandula spica*, which is said to be the Old English or Mitcham Lavender, a bush 3 to 4 feet in height with narrow grey leaves, and *L. vera*, described as the Dutch Lavender, which is said to be dwarfer, say 2 feet in height, and to have broader less silvery-grey leaves and slightly paler flowers. But the botanists will have none of it and say that *L. spica* and *L. vera* are simply synonyms for one original, *L. officinalis*.

It is much the same when one comes to the garden forms. These may be broadly divided into dwarf and tall, light coloured and dark coloured, but when it comes to detail it is difficult to sort some of them out. Hidcote and *nana atropurpurea* are both foot-high bushes with deep violet flowers and may well be identical, though some experts think there are slight differences which separate them. Munstead Dwarf and *nana* are also dwarf varieties about 1 foot high but not quite so dark in colour. The two names are probably applied to the same plant. Grappenhall Variety is 3 to 4 feet tall and a medium lavender colour. Twickle Purple is also a big bush, but differs in having darker coloured flowers. There is a white lavender named *alba* and one with flesh-pink flowers named *rosea*. Many more varieties will be found in the catalogues of specialists.

A quite distinct species which is worth planting is *L. stoechas* which makes a small bush, 12 to 18 inches high, with rather broad dense spikes of deep purple flowers with prominent purple bracts.

All these lavenders delight in well-drained soils and sunny places. They grow specially well on chalk or limestone but are not fussy about soil. *L. stoechas* should have a specially warm and sheltered position as it is a little tender. All varieties of *L. officinalis* benefit from being trimmed with shears after flowering to prevent them becoming straggly.

Lavenders can be increased by cuttings of firm young growth taken from June to August and rooted in a propagating frame or under mist, or by cuttings of fully ripe growth in September or October in a frame or sheltered position outdoors.

LAVATERA (Tree Mallow) Most lavateras grown in gardens are annuals but one, *Lavatera olbia*, is a rather soft-wooded shrub which will quickly make an open loosely branched bush to 6 feet high and rather more through. It has magenta or rose-pink flowers, produced from July to October, and grey-green leaves. The variety known as *rosea* is one of the most pleasing for colour. It thrives in well-drained soils and does well near the sea. This is not one of the choicest of shrubs but is useful for its speedy growth, late flowering and ability to thrive in quite poor soils. It is not, as a rule, long-lived but can be readily raised from seed sown in a frame or greenhouse in spring or by cuttings of young growth any time from June to September.

LEPTOSPERMUM (Manuka) Choice and beautiful evergreen shrubs with narrow heather-like leaves and small but abundant white, pink or carmine flowers in May and June. The species most commonly grown is *Leptospermum scoparium* which in mild districts will reach a height of 12 to 15 feet but is more commonly seen as a bush 8 to 10 feet high and rather less through. Typically it has white flowers but there are numerous forms, including *chapmanii* and *nichollsii*, both with deep carmine single flowers, *flore pleno*, with double white flowers, and Red Damask, with double carmine flowers.

All leptospermums like well-drained soils, preferably devoid of free lime. They will thrive under much the same conditions as rhododendrons and azaleas but prefer full sun to shade. They are not sufficiently hardy to be fully reliable in all parts of the country but are excellent for the milder counties. No pruning is required.

All can be increased by seed, which will often germinate freely around the bushes or can be sown in sandy peat in a greenhouse or frame in spring. Seedlings may vary in colour and selected garden varieties are grown from summer cuttings of firm young growth in a propagating frame or under mist.

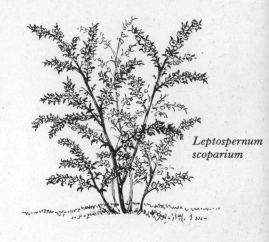

Leptospernum scoparium

LEUCOTHOË These evergreen shrubs, belonging to the heather family, are sometimes known as *Andromeda* and have the small white urn-shaped flowers of that genus. *Leucothoë catesbaei* grows from 3 to 6 feet high and spreads slowly by offsets rather like a herbaceous plant, so that in time it may become considerably broader than it is high. The stems arch and the small flowers, produced in May, hang on the under stems and may be partly hidden by the leaves. By contrast *L. davisiae*, a smaller shrub not exceeding 3 feet in height, carries its flowers aloft, in June, in short clustered spikes, so that they are more conspicuous.

In common with many other heather relations, the leucothoës do not like lime. They thrive in peaty or sandy soils and *L. catesbaei* will put up with a great deal of shade, which makes it a useful cover plant in woodland. No pruning is required.

Leucothoë catesbaei can be increased by division between October and April, *L. davisiae* by cuttings of firm young growth in July or August in a propagating frame or under mist.

Leucothoë catesbaei

LEYCESTERIA (Himalayan Honeysuckle) The semi-shrub *Leycesteria formosa* may in a hard winter be killed to ground level but will shoot up again from the base like a herbaceous plant. It looks very unlike a honeysuckle though it does belong to the same family. The stems are long, unbranched, green and cane-like and the claret-purple and white flowers hang in short trails in late summer. They are followed by dark purple berries. In good soil these stems may grow to 8 feet. The plant spreads slowly by offsets and may eventually become rather wider than it is high. It is all the better for being fairly drastically thinned each February or March, many of the older stems being cut right out but the best of the younger stems retained at full length. It is readily raised from seed, which often germinates all over the place as a result of berries being eaten by birds.

LIGUSTRUM (Privet) One species of privet, *Ligustrum ovalifolium*, has been used on such a vast scale as a hedge plant that it has tended to obscure the fact that there are other privets, some of greater merit. Nevertheless *L. ovalifolium* is an excellent shrub, quick growing, bushy, unfussy as regards soil or situation, thriving well in towns. Left to its own devices it will make a big bush, 15 feet high and as much through, with little clusters of white flowers in July. Yet it can be clipped to a height of 3 feet and breadth of 12 to 18 inches without in the least affecting its health or longevity. The golden-leaved form, *aureomarginatum*, is one of the most cheerful of shrubs and is at least equally popular for hedge making. It is slower growing and makes a smaller bush but otherwise is similar in every respect.

Another species which makes an excellent hedge is *L. ionandrum*. It is slower growing than *L. ovalifolium* but, left to its own devices, will eventually reach a height and spread of 6 to 8 feet. The leaves are much smaller than those of *L. ovalifolium*, the habit stiffer and more branching. There is some confusion about the naming of this species which is said by some authorities to be synonymous

Leycesteria formosa

Mahonia japonica

Mahonia aquifolium

Mahonia lomariifolia

Magnolia stellata

Mutisia retusa

Myrtus communis tarentina

Neillia longiracemosa

Cynthia Newsome-Taylor

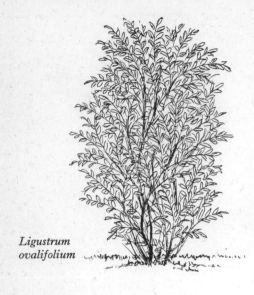

Ligustrum ovalifolium

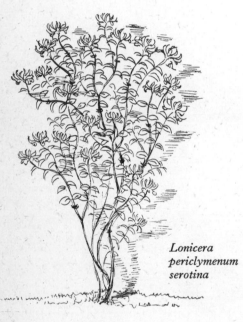

Lonicera periclymenum serotina

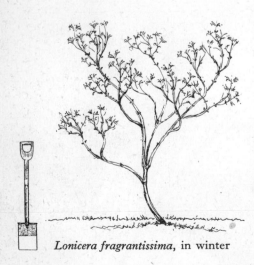

Lonicera fragrantissima, in winter

with *L. delavayanum* and *L. prattii* though others make these all distinct species.

There is no ambiguity about *L. japonicum* and *L. lucidum*, though they are closely allied. Both are evergreens with shining green leaves. Both have quite large sprays of white flowers in late summer and early autumn. But *L. japonicum* is a shrub of medium size, 6 to 8 feet high, whereas *L. lucidum* is much bigger and can reach tree-like proportions. There are variegated varieties of each and one form of *L. lucidum*, named *latifolium*, has leaves as large and stout as those of a camellia.

All these species and varieties of ligustrum can be grown in any reasonable soil and are not at all fussy. They will grow in full sun or shade and most are fully hardy, but *L. japonicum* may be damaged in severe winters. All can be pruned in spring and *L. ovalifolium* and *L. ionandrum* can be further pruned or clipped several times during the summer to make them into neat and tidy hedges.

All can be increased by cuttings, either taken in summer and rooted in a propagating frame or under mist, or in autumn or early spring and rooted in an ordinary frame or in a sheltered position in the open.

LONICERA (Honeysuckle, Woodbine) By no means all the loniceras are climbers, though many of the most popular are. The Common Honeysuckle or Woodbine of British hedgerows and woodlands is *Lonicera periclymenum*. In gardens it is usually represented by one of its forms, either the Early Dutch Honeysuckle, *belgica*, or the Late Dutch Honeysuckle, *serotina*. Both have larger and redder flowers than the type. The Early Dutch flowers in late May and June, the Late Dutch from July to September. Both are very vigorous twining climbers and both are deciduous.

Lonicera caprifolium is similar to *L. periclymenum* but the leaves around the flowers are united to clasp the stem. *L. japonica* is evergreen in a mild winter, though it may lose most of its leaves if the weather is severe. The flowers are not very showy but they are intensely fragrant and produced more or less continuously from midsummer to September. It has a most attractive variety, named *aureo-reticulata*, in which the leaves are netted with gold. Other forms of this honeysuckle are *flexuosa*, in which the flowers are tinged with red, and *halliana*, in which they commence by being white but become soft yellow with age.

Lonicera tragophylla has larger flowers than those of the Common Honeysuckle and they are bright yellow but they have no scent. The plant is deciduous, as is its hybrid *L. tellmanniana*, a very handsome but equally scentless climber with large yellow red-tipped flowers in June and July. Its other parent is *L. sempervirens*, known as the Trumpet Honeysuckle because of the size of its orange-red flowers, which also lack scent. Unfortunately this very handsome species is not fully hardy. *L. sempervirens* has produced another fine hybrid, named *L. brownii*, of which the best form is *fuchsioides*, the Scarlet Trumpet Honeysuckle, with orange-red flowers all summer.

Lonicera etrusca is deciduous or semi-evergreen according to the severity of the weather and it has very fine fragrant yellow flowers in June and July. It is not very hardy but with *L. caprifolium* it has produced a hardier hybrid which is about as handsome. This is correctly named *L. americana*, but is sometimes called *L. italica* or *L. grata*, and it has big fragrant yellow and red flowers produced all the summer.

Lonicera henryi is evergreen, has small purple flowers and is not unlike *L. giraldii*, another honeysuckle which will make a dense tangle of growth.

In general the bush honeysuckles are less showy in flower but several of them flower in winter and one, *L. nitida*, is an evergreen of dense habit which stands clipping well and makes an excellent hedge up to about 5 feet.

Two of the best winter-flowering bush honeysuckles are *L. fragrantissima* and *L. standishii*, both 6 to 8 feet high and rather more through, semi-evergreen with very fragrant creamy flowers from December to February. The two have produced a hybrid, named *L. purpusii*, which is more effective than either.

All these honeysuckles, climbers and bushes alike, enjoy good loamy soils but can be grown almost anywhere in sun or partial shade. When overgrown the climbers can be thinned and reduced in February or March. *L. nitida* can be clipped repeatedly in summer without harm.

Climbing honeysuckles will often layer themselves, and can be increased by this means, but all honeysuckles can be raised from cuttings of firm young growth in summer in a propagating frame or under mist.

LUPINUS (Tree Lupin) There is an excellent evergreen shrubby species of lupin named *Lupinus arboreus*. It grows rapidly into a big loose bush 6 to 8 feet high and as much or more through. The flowers are borne in spikes like those of the herbaceous lupin but are smaller, white, cream or yellow and fragrant. They are at their best in June and July. It is not a long-lived shrub but it usually regenerates itself by seed and can be very readily raised by this means. However, seedlings may show some variation of flower colour and selected forms should be increased by cuttings of firm young growth at almost any time in spring or summer in a frame. Stems can be shortened after the flowers fade to prevent plants from becoming straggly. Lupins do specially well in sandy soil and are fine seaside shrubs but they are not fussy about soil so long as it is reasonably well-drained.

Lupinus arboreus

LYCIUM (Box Thorn) The species commonly grown, *Lycium chinense*, is a loosely branched, thin stemmed, rather sprawling shrub chiefly of value because it will grow in the poorest of sandy soils and withstand sea gales. It is, in consequence, a useful shrub as a shelter belt for seaside gardens. It will reach a height of 8 or 10 feet and may be more through. The small purple flowers (pink in variety *carnosum*), produced in summer, are not showy but are followed by orange-red berries which can be quite attractive. Overgrown plants can be cut back in spring. Propagation is by seed sown in greenhouse or frame in spring, by cuttings of firm young growth in a frame in summer, or by ripe cuttings in October in a sheltered place and sandy soil outdoors.

MAGNOLIA Most of the magnolias are trees but one which is of shrub-like height and habit is *Magnolia stellata*. This is deciduous and makes a well branched bush 8 to 12 feet high and tending to become broader than this with age. The white flowers have narrower petals than those of most magnolias and they appear early, starting to open in March and continuing into April. There is a form, named *rosea*, with pale pink flowers. *M. stellata* likes peaty soil, though it will grow in a considerable variety of soils so long as they are not strongly alkaline. It should be grown in a sunny but reasonably sheltered position because, though quite hardy, its flowers are liable to be spoiled by frost. No pruning is required. Plants can be raised by layering the younger branches in spring or early summer or from seed sown in peaty soil in a greenhouse. Nurserymen sometimes graft on to seedlings of other magnolias of which seed is more readily available.

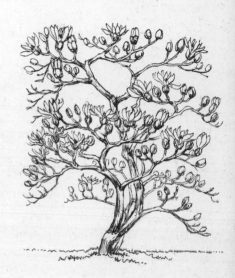

Magnolia stellata

MAHONIA At one time these evergreen shrubs were known as *Berberis* but they differ so much from the familiar Barberries that for once the gardener can feel thankful that botanists have placed them in a separate genus. All have leaves composed of numerous leaflets, which individually often have some resemblance to the leaves of holly. Indeed the commonest of all mahonias is called *Mahonia aquifolium*, the same specific name as that of the common holly which is *Ilex aquifolium*. It means a leaf with points or spikes. This is a very good shrub, with shining lustrous-green leaves which turn red or purple in autumn, clusters of golden-yellow flowers from February to the end of April, followed by plum-purple berries. It grows 3 to 4 feet high but may spread over a considerably greater area as it throws out suckers which gradually increases its girth. There is a beautiful form of this mahonia, named *undulata*, which is rather taller (it may reach 6 feet) and has leaves which are waved and are even glossier than those of the type.

Mahonia aquifolium

There has been confusion between two fine species named *M. japonica* and *M. bealei* as at one time their names became reversed, the plant properly called

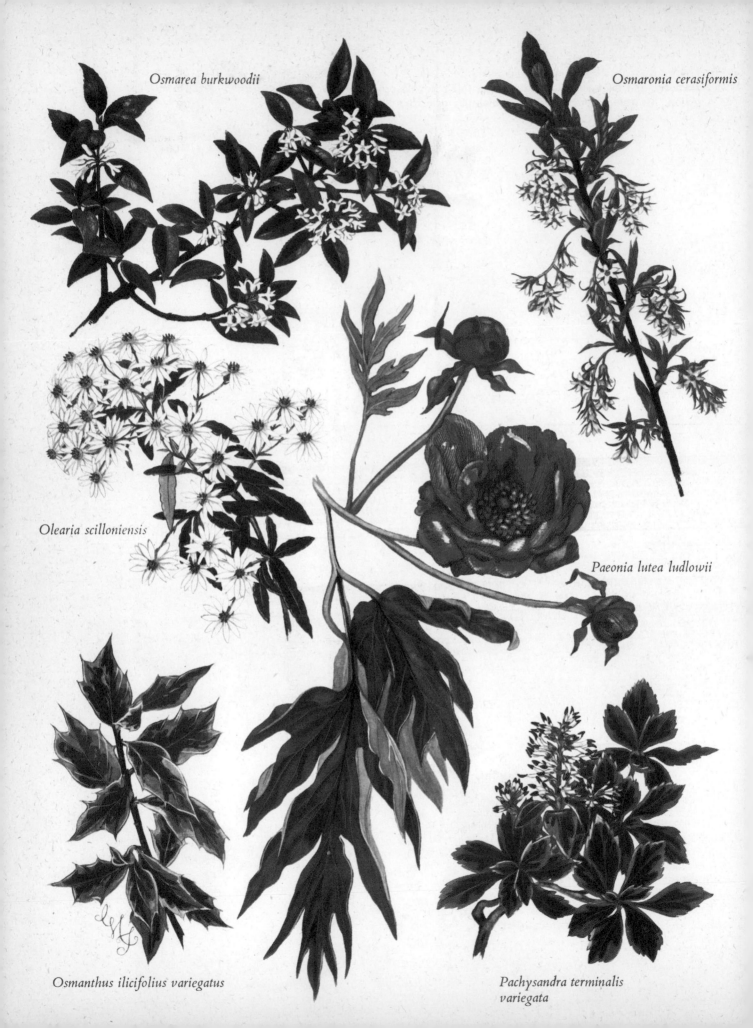

Osmarea burkwoodii

Osmaronia cerasiformis

Olearia scilloniensis

Paeonia lutea ludlowii

Osmanthus ilicifolius variegatus

Pachysandra terminalis variegata

Paeonia suffruticosa

Paeonia delavayi

Cynthia Newsome-Taylor

Mahonia
lomariifolia

Mutisia
oligodon

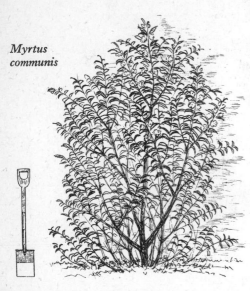

Myrtus
communis

M. japonica becoming known as *M. bealei* and vice-versa. When ordering it is well to bear this in mind and make quite certain that the nurseryman has his names right and knows which plant is which. For of the two *M. japonica* is the more effective garden shrub, growing 5 to 7 feet high and as much as 12 feet through and carrying its fragrant lemon-yellow flowers in long trails or spikes spread out like the spokes of a wheel. The leaves are also arranged in big whorls and are very long, composed of as many as 15 leaflets. This mahonia may commence to open its flowers in December or January but is normally at its best in February and early March. *M. bealei* is similar in habit but its flower spikes are shorter and held more erect in the form of a shuttlecock.

The most handsome of all in leaf is *M. lomariifolia* but it suffers from the drawback that it is apt to make a rather 'leggy' plant, not much branched, with stiffly erect stems attaining almost tree-like proportions with age, and with most of its leaves and flowers on top. The leaves are of the largest size, carried in whorls like those of *M. japonica* but longer and with even more leaflets. The yellow flowers are borne in semi-erect spikes arranged in similar shuttlecock fashion to those of *M. bealei* but longer. They come in winter and early spring.

There are other species such as *M. napaulensis*, a little like *M. japonica* but less handsome; *M. pinnata*, in the style of *M. aquifolium* but without the shine on its leaves; and *M. repens*, a useful ground cover shrub about 1 foot high but spreading indefinitely by underground stems or suckers. This has yellow flowers in May followed by dark purple berries.

Mahonias will grow in a great variety of soils and situations but some, such as *M. bealei*, *M. japonica*, *M. lomariifolia* and *M. napaulensis*, are a little tender and appreciate sheltered positions. Some, such as *M. aquifolium*, will grow well in quite dense shade and all will put up with some shade. As a rule pruning is unnecessary but plants can be cut back moderately after flowering and *M. aquifolium* is occasionally used as a hedge plant when it must be trimmed two or three times during late spring and summer.

Those that make underground stems or suckers can be increased by digging these out in autumn or late winter with roots attached or by lifting a plant and dividing it. All can be raised from cuttings of firm young growth in summer in a propagating frame or under mist, and also from seed sown in a frame or greenhouse in spring.

MUTISIA Very beautiful, but rather tender, climbing plants with showy daisy-type flowers. They are not very vigorous plants but in favourable places may reach a height of 8 or 10 feet, climbing by means of tendrils. *Mutisia decurrens* has orange or red flowers as large as those of an *Ursinia* or *Dimorphotheca* which they somewhat resemble. *M. oligodon*, *M. retusa* and *M. ilicifolia* have pink or mauve flowers. All bloom in summer.

These are difficult plants to establish outdoors, yet where they succeed they often grow freely for many years, spreading by means of suckers. They are most suitable for sheltered places in the South-west and West, in reasonably good well-drained soil. No pruning should be required. They can be raised from seed, sown in a warm greenhouse in spring, or by suckers detached with roots in autumn or early spring.

MYRTUS (Myrtle) The myrtles are fragrant both in flower and, when bruised or brushed, in leaf. They are beautiful evergreens and some have handsome peeling bark, but all are more or less tender so they cannot be grown reliably outdoors in Britain except in the milder parts of the country, *e.g.* near the sea and in the South and West. The Common Myrtle, *Myrtus communis*, will make a shrub 10 feet tall (rather more against a wall) and perhaps 7 or 8 feet through. The small white flowers are very freely produced in July. The leaves of the typical form are pointed but there are numerous forms and one, named *buxifolia*, has rounded leaves like a box. Another, *microphylla*, has smaller leaves than normal and a third, *tarentina*, is lower growing, more dense and has narrower leaves. Other forms will be found in nursery catalogues.

Myrtus ugni is a bigger shrub or small tree, rather round in habit with much thicker leaves and pink flowers.

These and other myrtles should be planted in good well-drained soil and sheltered but sunny positions. If necessary they can be pruned after flowering to restrict their size. All can be increased by seed sown in a warm greenhouse in spring, or by cuttings of firm young growth in summer in a propagating frame or under mist with soil warming.

NEILLIA Graceful deciduous shrubs of which the only species commonly found in British gardens is *Neillia longiracemosa*. This will grow 6 to 8 feet high and as much through and has erect slender stems bearing, in May and June, little semi-pendant trails of rosy-pink flowers. It is a graceful and distinctive shrub easily grown in any soil that is not liable to dry out badly in summer. No regular pruning is required but bushes can be thinned or reduced if desired after flowering. Cuttings of firm young growth will root readily in June or July in a propagating frame or under mist.

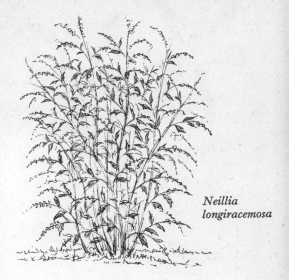

Neillia longiracemosa

OLEARIA (Daisy Bush, Tree Daisy) This is a big genus of evergreen shrubs many of which are very decorative but unfortunately few are reliably hardy. One of the exceptions is *Olearia haastii*, a densely branched rounded bush 6 to 8 feet high and about as much through, with neat rounded leaves which are green above and grey beneath, and abundant small white daisy flowers in July and August. It succeeds very well near the sea and also in towns, where it seems to be impervious to the most grime-laden atmosphere.

More distinguished in appearance but less hardy is *O. stellulata*, also known as *O. gunniana*. It is more open in habit, has small greyish leaves and white flowers which are produced very freely. There are also forms of this olearia with coloured flowers, blue, lavender or rose. This fine species grows 4 or 5 feet high and as much, or rather more, through and it flowers in May. So does *scilloniensis*, a hybrid between *O. stellulata* and *O. lyrata*, much like the former in appearance but reputed to be a little hardier. However it can be killed outright in a hard winter.

Olearia macrodonta has large leaves, not unlike those of a holly, and in mild districts it is sometimes used as a hedge plant. Left to its own devices it makes a very big bush 15 feet or more high and 10 or 12 feet through. It carries large clusters of white flowers in June. *O. ilicifolia* resembles it except that the leaves are much narrower.

Olearia macrodonta

All like well-drained soils and sunny positions. They thrive near the sea and *O. macrodonta* makes a useful windbreak in such places. It will stand being pruned to shape every year immediately after flowering. All can be raised from cuttings of firm young growth in summer in a propagating frame or under mist.

OSMANTHUS Evergreen shrubs with small flowers which are usually white and fragrant in the species commonly grown in British gardens. The shrub which most gardeners will think of first when *Osmanthus* is mentioned has been removed by botanists to another genus. Once known as *Osmanthus delavayi* this has now been renamed *Siphonosmanthus delavayi* and will be found described under that name. This leaves *O. ilicifolius*, also known as *O. aquifolium*, as the most popular species that is truly an *Osmanthus*. It is a big shrub, closely resembling a holly in growth and leaf, often 15 to 20 feet high and from 10 to 12 feet through, with small, white fragrant flowers in September and October. It has numerous garden varieties, one, named *purpurascens*, with young shoots and leaves purple; another, named *myrtifolius*, which has leaves without spines; two more, named *aureo-marginatus* and *argenteo-marginatus* or *variegatus*, with leaves variegated, the one with yellow, the other with silver.

Another striking species with larger thicker more leathery leaves is *O. armatus*. The flowers appear in autumn and are small, creamy-white and fragrant. It is 8 to 12 feet high and rather less through.

These and other species will grow in any reasonably good soil. They may be planted in full sun or partial shade. Pruning is not essential but they can be

Olearia scilloniensis

Periploca graeca

Parthenocissus henryana

Passiflora caerulea

Parthenocissus tricuspidata

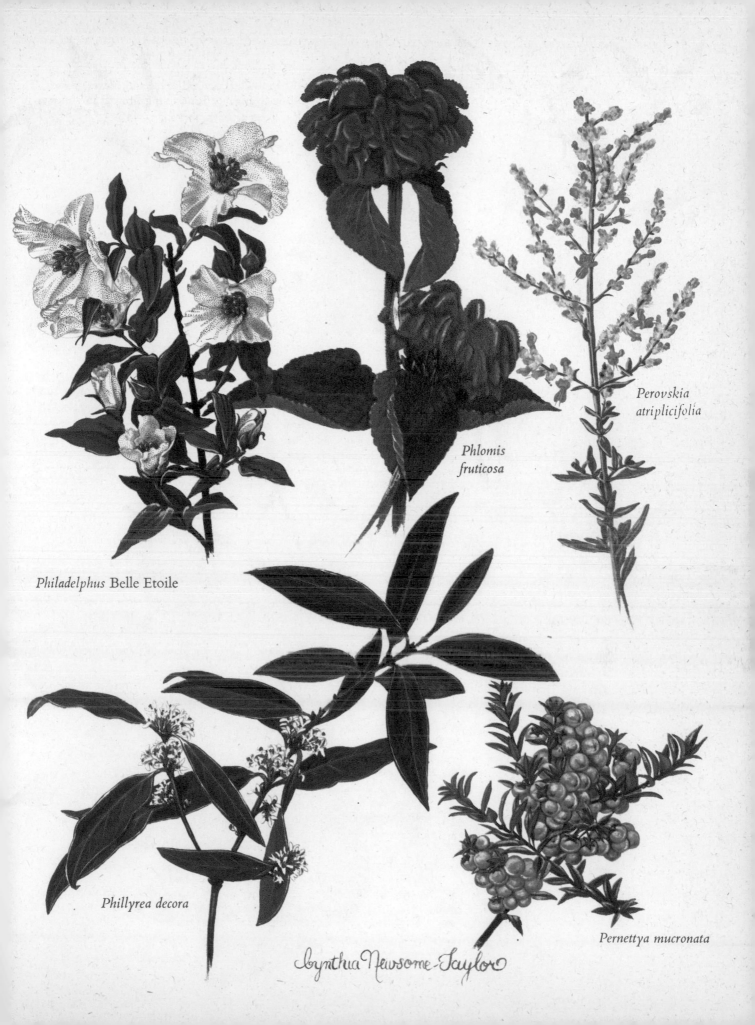

Phlomis
fruticosa

Perovskia
atriplicifolia

Philadelphus Belle Etoile

Phillyrea decora

Pernettya mucronata

Cynthia Newsome-Taylor

Osmaronia cerasiformis

Paeonia lutea ludlowii

Paeonia suffruticosa

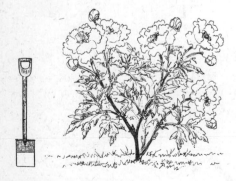

shortened or thinned, if desired, in spring or summer. Propagation is by cuttings of firm young growth in July or August in a propagating frame or under mist with soil warming.

OSMAREA This name is used to describe a hybrid between two shrubs belonging to different genera, *Siphonosmanthus delavayi* (better known as *Osmanthus delavayi*) and *Phillyrea decora*. This was made by a Mr Burkwood and so, to commemorate him, it is known as *Osmarea burkwoodii*. It is an excellent evergreen, 7 to 9 feet high and slightly less through, with small, neat, shining green leaves and small, white, fragrant flowers in late spring. It is densely branched and can be used as a hedge or it can be grown as a bush. It is not fussy about soil, will thrive in sun or partial shade and can be clipped or pruned several times in summer without harm. It is easily increased by summer cuttings of firm young growth in a propagating frame or under mist.

OSMARONIA (Osoberry) The deciduous shrub now known as *Osmaronia cerasiformis* is more familiar to gardeners under its old name *Nuttallia cerasiformis*. It is not particularly showy but useful because it flowers in February and March. It grows 6 or 8 feet high and may become broader than that by throwing up more and more stems around the base, rather like a black currant. The flowers, greenish-white or creamy-white and fragrant, are produced in little slender trails. They may be followed by purple fruits.

It is easily grown in any ordinary soil and sunny or partially shady place. It needs no pruning but if it becomes too big it can be thinned or cut back after flowering. It can be increased by digging out rooted suckers in autumn or winter or by seed sown in a greenhouse or frame in spring.

PACHYSANDRA Prostrate evergreen shrubs valuable as ground cover because they will thrive in dense shade. The species commonly grown is *Pachysandra terminalis* which in its common form has bright green leaves but it also has a more attractive variety, known as *variegata*, in which the leaves are broadly banded with silver. The small greenish flowers, produced in later winter, have no beauty. These shrubs do not exceed 8 inches in height but will continue to spread indefinitely. They thrive in any reasonable soil and prefer shady to sunny places. They can be increased by cuttings of young growth from June to August in a frame or under mist.

PAEONIA (Peony) Many peonies are herbaceous plants but there are also very decorative shrubby kinds, all deciduous, of which one, *Paeonia suffruticosa*, has produced numerous garden varieties. These are ordinarily known as Tree Peonies, have very large flowers, single, semi-double or fully double and in a considerable range of colours from white, through pink, rose and carmine, to crimson and purple, often with striking markings or blotches of maroon. All grow rather slowly into quite large, rather open bushes, eventually 4 or 5 feet high and nearly as much through. They flower in May and June.

Paeonia lutea is only partly shrubby, tending to die back to woody basal stems in winter. It grows 3 feet high and has yellow flowers in May. It has been crossed with *P. suffruticosa* to increase the colour range of the Tree Peonies to include yellow and orange and these hybrids are usually listed under the name *P. lemoinei*.

Paeonia lutea ludlowii grows more rapidly into a bigger woodier bush, 6 or 7 feet high, with long stems radiating in the form of a shuttlecock but there is considerable confusion between this plant and *P. lutea* and probably there are intermediate forms in gardens. Its cup-shaped flowers are yellow and come in May and the deeply divided leaves make this bush a handsome object all summer. Rather similar in leaf and habit, but not above 5 feet in height, is *P. delavayi* which has flatter, more saucer-shaped flowers of deepest crimson in May.

All these shrubby peonies like good rich soils and the garden varieties of *P. suffruticosa* can be topdressed each spring with decayed manure or compost to keep them in full vigour. They like sunny but fairly sheltered positions and are not well adapted to fend for themselves in the competitive atmosphere of the shrub border. No pruning is required. The species can be raised readily from seed sown in greenhouse or frame in spring but the garden varieties will not breed true from seed and should be layered in early spring. Nurserymen often graft them on to roots of herbaceous peonies but this is not very desirable. If such plants are put in a little deeply, with 4 or 5 inches of soil over the roots, they will probably in time make stem roots of their own which is an advantage.

PARTHENOCISSUS (Virginia Creeper) These are the deciduous climbing plants more familiar to gardeners under their old names *Ampelopsis* and *Vitis*. There is considerable confusion about their correct naming and in nursery catalogues they are most likely to be included with other ornamental vines under *Vitis*.

The very popular self-clinging Virginia Creeper, which usually passes in catalogues as *Vitis inconstans*, is in fact *Parthenocissus tricuspidata; veitchii* and *lowii* are small-leaved forms of this species. The large-leaved or true Virginia Creeper is generally called *Vitis quinquefolia* in gardens but is really *Parthenocissus quinquefolia*, and the very beautiful but slightly tender kind with velvet-green leaves netted with white above and flushed with purple beneath is not *Vitis henryana*, as most of the catalogues say, but *Parthenocissus henryana*.

These are all vigorous self-clinging climbers that will quickly cover a wall with a dense network of slender growths and handsome green leaves which change to shades of scarlet and crimson before they fall in autumn. They will grow practically anywhere in any reasonable soil, but colour best if exposed to the sun. If they grow too large, as well they may, they can be cut back drastically in late winter or early spring. They can be increased in many ways; from seed, when available, sown in a greenhouse in spring, by layering in summer or, most commonly, by cuttings of young growth in summer in a propagating frame or under mist.

PASSIFLORA (Passion Flower) Most of the Passion Flowers are too tender to be grown outdoors in Britain but one, *Passiflora caerulea*, thrives well in the milder counties of the West and South-west and is so fast growing that it is worth trying in sheltered sunny places in many other parts of the country. It will survive some frost and even if it disappears in a hard winter it can be replanted in the spring and will soon cover its allotted space once more. It climbs by means of tendrils and, against a wall, will soon reach a height of 15 feet or more. In the typical form the flowers are white and blue, but there is also a lovely variety, named Constance Elliott, with white flowers. Both bloom more or less continuously from midsummer to early autumn. They are not at all fussy about soil, but will grow most vigorously in a good loamy soil. They should have a sunny position and the only pruning required is to cut out weather-damaged growth in April. The blue and white type can be increased from seed sown in a warm greenhouse in spring, but the white-flowered form will not breed true from seed and must be increased by cuttings of young growth in summer in a propagating frame or under mist.

PERIPLOCA (Silk Vine) These very vigorous twining plants are only suitable for planting outdoors in the mildest parts of the country, as they will not survice much frost. The species most likely to be grown in Britain is *Periploca graeca*, which has clusters of greenish-yellow and purplish-brown heavily-scented flowers, more curious than beautiful. It likes a warm sunny position and well-drained soil and can be raised from seed sown in a warm greenhouse in spring, by layering in spring or early summer, or by cuttings of young growth in summer in a propagating frame or under mist with soil warming.

PERNETTYA This is one of the showiest of dwarf evergreen berry-bearing shrubs because its berries are so freely produced and are of so many different colours, some of them rather unusual. The species grown is *Pernettya mucronata*, which is said to reach a height of 5 feet on occasion but is more usually seen at about half that height, though spreading more or less indefinitely by suckers. The leaves are small firm and shining, the flowers small but numerous, bell-shaped

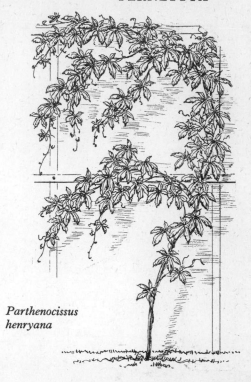

Parthenocissus henryana

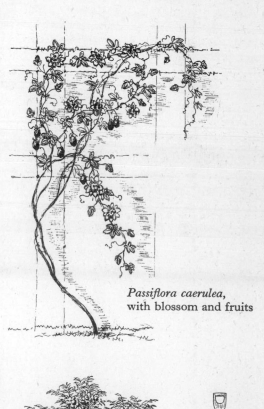

Passiflora caerulea, with blossom and fruits

Pernettya mucronata

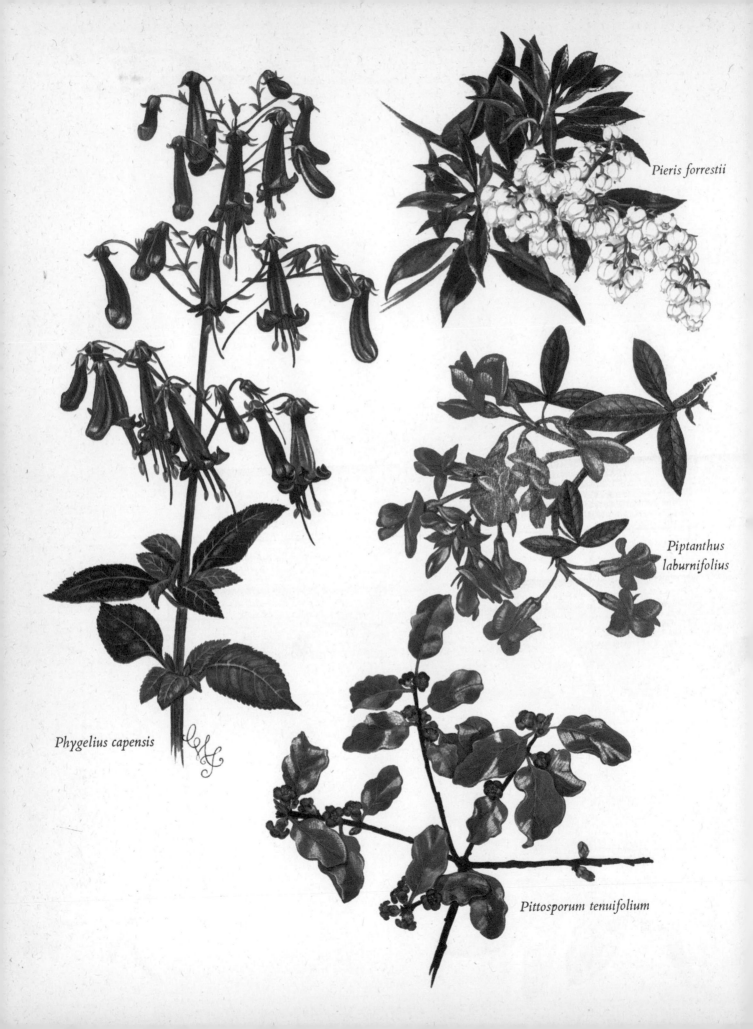

Pieris forrestii

*Piptanthus
laburnifolius*

Phygelius capensis

Pittosporum tenuifolium

Pittosporum tenuifolium Silver Queen

Polygonum baldschuanicum

Poncirus trifoliata

Pittosporum tobira

Cynthia Newsome-Taylor

Perovskia atriplicifolia

Philadelphus coronarius

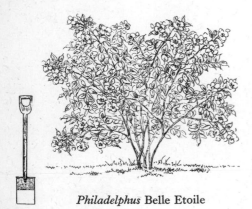

Philadelphus Belle Etoile

like those of a heather, white or tinged with pink. They are quite attractive in May and June but it is the large berries that follow in late summer and autumn that make this shrub so very worth while. They may be white, pink, lilac, rose, purple or dark red and they remain for a long time.

Pernettyas like sunny places, but soils not liable to dry out severely in summer, a combination that can only be assured by mixing plenty of humus-forming material with the soil, *e.g.* peat, leafmould or compost. They need no pruning.

As they spread by suckers or offsets, they can usually be increased readily by division in autumn or late winter. Seed can be sown in peaty soil in frame or greenhouse in spring, and cuttings of firm young growth can also be rooted in summer in a propagating frame or under mist.

PEROVSKIA (Afghan Sage) The name of this shrub is also frequently spelled *Perowskia*. The species commonly grown is *Perovskia atriplicifolia*. It makes woody stems at the base and from these annually throws up strong young stems 3 or 4 feet long, but these stems do not themselves become woody and permanent. Instead they die back or become damaged in winter, so that the species behaves as part shrub, part herbaceous plant. The small lavender-blue flowers are borne in long slender spikes in August and September, at which season the whole plant has somewhat the appearance of an unusually large and attenuated lavender, an impression further fostered by the grey stems and leaves. This is a good shrub for a warm sunny position in well-drained soil. Each March or April the previous year's growth, or what is left of it, should be cut back to within an inch or so of the older and woodier basal branches. Propagation is by cuttings of the young growth in June or July in a propagating frame or under mist, preferably with soil warming.

PHILADELPHUS (Mock Orange, Syringa) These beautiful summer-flowering deciduous shrubs have been so greatly developed by gardeners that the garden-raised varieties and hybrids have become more important than the species. Of the latter, the most important for garden display are *Philadelphus coronarius*, with heavily scented creamy-white flowers; *P. grandiflorus*, with large pure white scentless flowers, and *P. microphyllus*, with pure white pleasantly fragrant flowers. The first two are big, growing from 10 to 15 feet high and often being nearly as much through, but *P. microphyllus* is smaller, a densely twiggy bush seldom above 4 feet high and 5 or 6 feet through.

Philadelphus microphyllus and *P. coronarius* together have produced a first-class hybrid named *P. lemoinei*, a 6-foot bush with abundant white fragrant flowers in June. This hybrid has, in turn, been used with other species, including a rather tender Mexican kind named *P. coulteri* which has purple blotches on its white petals, to produce a whole series of delightful varieties which are amongst the best of early-summer-flowering shrubs. There are so many of these, some closely alike, that it is best to make a selection from plants in bloom. A few that are specially recommended are Beauclerk, with very large single flowers, white with a flush of purple at the centre; Belle Etoile, rather similar but with a more pronounced purple blotch at the base of each petal; Sybille, with similar flowers to the last but making a smaller bush, around 3 feet high and 4 or 5 feet through, and Virginal, with large double white flowers. All are deliciously scented.

The species and hybrids of *Philadelphus* are all very easy to grow in almost any soil and reasonably open position. All can be pruned immediately after flowering, when the stems that are bearing the faded flowers can be cut out as far as non-flowering stems or young shoots. By this means bushes can be kept well below their maximum size and the quality of the flowers improved.

Propagation is easy, either by cuttings of firm young growth from June to August in a propagating frame or under mist, or by cuttings of fully ripe growth in October out of doors in sandy soil and a sheltered place.

PHILLYREA Evergreen shrubs or small trees, the best of which for garden decoration is *Phillyrea decora*. This makes a rounded rather wide bush, 7 or

8 feet high when fully grown and as much as 9 or 10 feet through, with leathery shining dark green leaves and clusters of small white fragrant flowers in April, followed by blackberry-like fruits. It is quite hardy and easily grown in almost any soil and sunny or partially shady position. It can be cut back moderately each spring, if desired, but pruning is not essential. It is readily raised from seed sown in a frame or greenhouse in spring, or by cuttings of firm young growth in June or July in a propagating frame or under mist.

PHLOMIS (Jerusalem Sage) Handsome evergreen shrubs with sage-like leaves and whorls of hooded yellow flowers in June and July. The species most commonly grown, *Phlomis fruticosa*, has grey leaves and makes a rather broad bush, 3 feet high and as much as 5 feet through. It is attractive in foliage as well as in flower. *P. chrysophylla* is very similar but there is a slight yellowish tinge to the grey leaves which gives them a distinctive appearance.

Both are shrubs for warm sunny places and well-drained soils. They may be damaged by frost in severe winters, but are seldom killed outright, unless planted in very exposed places or on winter-wet soils. They can become a little straggly with age, a tendency which can be prevented by trimming them over lightly after flowering. They can be raised from seed sown in a greenhouse in spring, or by cuttings of firm young growth any time in summer in a propagating frame or under mist.

PHYGELIUS (Cape Fuchsia) The only species commonly grown, *Phygelius capensis*, is a highly distinctive plant, half shrub, half herbaceous plant, which in cold places will be killed to ground level every winter but will shoot up again in the spring. In milder climates it will make some kind of permanent woody framework, though much of the young growth may die back annually. Planted against a sheltered wall, it may behave like a climber, ascending to a height of 8 to 10 feet, but in the open it is unlikely to exceed 3 to 4 feet. The flowers are scarlet, narrowly tubular and with the curious appearance of being upside-down. They are carried in a loose spray in late summer and early autumn. *P. capensis* likes warm sunny places and well-drained soils. It can be increased by seed sown in spring in a warm greenhouse, by layers in spring or summer, or by cuttings in summer in a propagating frame.

PIERIS Evergreen shrubs with sprays of white flowers, superficially rather like lily-of-the-valley. They belong to the heather family and thrive under similar conditions to these and rhododendrons. *Pieris floribunda* is one of the smallest and hardiest, a well-branched dome-shaped shrub 3 to 5 feet high and about as much through, producing its flowers in rather stiff sprays in March and April. *P. japonica* is larger and more graceful, 8 or 9 feet high and as much as 12 feet through, with flowers produced in arching sprays. *P. forrestii* has much the same habit and dimensions but is a little later and not usually quite so free-flowering, for which it makes ample amends by producing young shoots and leaves which are bright red and pink. In spring this is one of the most spectacular evergreens. *P. taiwanensis* also has red young growths, but not so brightly coloured as those of *P. forrestii*. It makes a fine bush, 6 to 8 feet high and 8 or 9 feet through, with spreading sprays of white flowers in March and April. *P. formosa* is the last to bloom, in May, and has the largest individual flowers, but is also the least hardy.

All need lime-free soils, preferably with peat or leafmould. They will grow in sun but prefer a little shade, such as in thin woodland. They will benefit from annual topdressing with peat to keep the roots cool and moist. No pruning is required but it is an advantage to remove the faded flowers and so prevent seeding.

Pieris can be raised from seed sown in sandy peat in a frame or greenhouse in spring, or by layering young branches in spring or early summer.

PIPTANTHUS (Evergreen Laburnum) The only species grown, *Piptanthus laburnifolius*, also known as *P. nepalensis*, is not fully hardy and in a cold place will lose all its leaves in winter and may even be partially killed. But in warmer

Phlomis fruticosa

Pieris forrestii

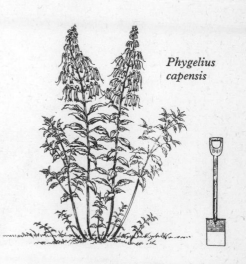

Phygelius capensis

93

Pyracantha Waterer's Orange

Pyracantha atalantioides
(flowers)

Potentilla fruticosa
Primrose Beauty

Pyracantha
coccinea
lalandii

Pyracantha atalantioides (fruits)

Potentilla fruticosa
Jackman's Variety

Prunus lusitanica

Prunus glandulosa albiplena

Prunus tenella gessleriana

Prunus incisa

Prunus laurocerasus

Cynthia Newsome-Taylor

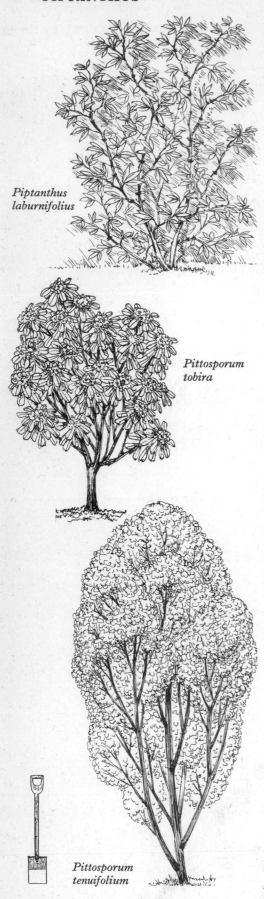

Piptanthus laburnifolius

Pittosporum tobira

Pittosporum tenuifolium

conditions it is evergreen or partially so and, as its leaves and flowers look a little like those of a laburnum, the name Evergreen Laburnum is not inapt. However the yellow pea-type flowers are not borne in long trails like those of a laburnum, but in short erect spikes which are at their best in May. It likes a warm sunny place and well-drained soil and may be trained against a wall, though it is really a bush with rather strong cane-like stems which may reach a height of 8 to 12 feet. The only pruning necessary is the removal of frost-damaged growth in April. It is readily increased from seed which often germinates freely around the plant, but it is best to grow the seedlings on in pots until large enough for planting as they resent root breakage.

PITTOSPORUM   Evergreen shrubs grown primarily for the beauty of their foliage, though the white, cream, yellow or purple flowers are pleasantly fragrant. All are rather tender. The most popular are *Pittosporum tenuifolium* and *P. tobira*. The former will grow to tree-like size but can easily be kept much smaller by pruning and in the South-west is often used as a hedge plant. The twigs are black and the small rounded leaves are a light shining green. Great quantities of the young stems are cut and sold in the flower markets of Britain as foliage. There is a variety, named Silver Queen, the leaves of which are variegated with silver.

Pittosporum tobira has stouter growth, larger leaves and a more freely branched habit. It is said to grow to a height of 70 feet or more in China and Japan, where it is native, but in Britain is commonly seen as a rounded bush 8 to 10 feet high and as much through. The flowers are creamy-white, more conspicuous than those of most species, very fragrant and produced in April and May.

These and other species of pittosporum should be given warm and sheltered positions. They like reasonably good well-drained soils and do extremely well near the sea, appearing to be unharmed even by quite a lot of salt spray.

They can be increased by seed sown in a warm greenhouse in spring, or by cuttings of firm young growth in summer in a propagating frame or under mist, preferably with soil warming.

POLYGONUM (Russian Vine)   Most of the polygonums are herbaceous plants but one, *Polygonum baldschuanicum*, is a very vigorous, quick-growing woody climbing plant. It ascends by twining and will quickly get to the top of a sizeable tree or cover a whole wall or outhouse with a tangled mass of growth from which, in July, will erupt great foaming sprays of small creamy-white or pinkish-white bloom, to remain throughout August and September. It is valuable because of the speed with which it will produce an effect and for its own considerable beauty in bloom. It thrives in almost any soil and sunny or partially shady position. It can be increased from cuttings, but these are not among the easiest to root. They should be taken in July or August, prepared from firm young growth pulled off with a heel of older wood. The base of the cutting should be dipped in rooting power and inserted in a propagating frame or under mist with soil warming.

PONCIRUS (Hardy Orange)   Only one species is grown and this has suffered from a plethora of names, having been known as *Citrus trifoliata*, *Aegle sepiaria* and now as *Poncirus trifoliata*. It is a deciduous shrub, rather stiff and angular in its branching, 6 or 8 feet high and at least as much through, armed with strong spines, with fragrant white flowers in May followed by small aromatic orange-like fruits. It is reasonably hardy and likes a warm sunny position. It will thrive in any reasonably good soil and is increased by seed sown in a warm greenhouse in spring.

POTENTILLA (Shrubby Cinquefoil)   Deciduous shrubs of considerable beauty which flower more or less continuously all through the summer. All the garden varieties, of which there are many, are derived from one species, *Potentilla fruticosa*, a densely branched bush 3 or 4 feet high and as much or rather more through, with yellow flowers from May to September. The garden forms vary in habit and colour. *Arbuscula* is very broad and spreading but rather short and the flowers are primrose-yellow, whereas *friedrichsenii* may reach a height of 6 feet and also has light yellow flowers. Jackman's Variety has flowers of superior size and deep golden-yellow colour; *vilmoriniana* has silvery leaves and cream-coloured flowers and *veitchii* has white flowers. Many more will be found in catalogues.

All like sunny places and well-drained soils and all will benefit from some thinning or cutting back each March as there is a tendency for the older stems to die out. All the best of the younger growth should be retained. Propagation is by cuttings of firm young growth in summer in a propagating frame or under mist.

PRUNUS This great genus includes all the cherries, almonds and plums, many of which are splendid ornamental plants but, as they are trees, beyond the scope of this book. There are, however, a few notable exceptions. The Cherry Laurel is *Prunus laurocerasus*, tree-like under some conditions but often used as a hedge or screening shrub and also capable of making a shrubby specimen of considerable beauty. Treated in this way, with a little pruning to keep it within bounds, it will make a big well-branched bush, 10 to 15 feet high and as much or more through, with large shining evergreen leaves and spikes of small fragrant white flowers in May. It has a number of varieties differing mainly in the size and shape of their leaves; for instance, *caucasica* has very long pointed leaves, *schipkaensis* narrow leaves and *rotundifolia* rather rounder leaves and a shorter more compact habit.

Another very useful evergreen species is the Portugal Laurel, *Prunus lusitanica*. This also stands pruning well and is used for hedges and windbreaks and sometimes to make topiary specimens. The leaves are pointed and dark green, the habit bushy, height 10 to 15 feet and spread as much as 20 feet. Much smaller plants can be maintained by pruning. The flower spikes are similar to those of *P. laurocerasus*.

Prunus cistena is a hybrid plum with purple leaves which grows only a few feet high and can be pruned to make a dwarf hedge.

Prunus glandulosa albiplena is a popular early-flowering shrub, usually referred to as an almond though it is more nearly allied to the cherries. It grows 4 or 5 feet tall, making slender stems clad for a considerable part of their length with double white flowers in April. There is also another form, known as *sinensis* or *roseo-plena*, which has double pink flowers.

Prunus incisa is known as the Fuji Cherry and make a big bush, 10 to 12 feet high and as much as 15 to 20 feet through, smothered in March with small single pale pink flowers.

Prunus triloba plena is an almond, 7 or 8 feet high and as much through, with slender stems wreathed in quite large double pink flowers in March and April. It needs a warm sheltered place. *P. tenella* is also an almond, 3 or 4 feet high and 5 or 6 feet through, with single pink flowers in April. It has a white-flowered form named *alba* and also one with carmine flowers named *gessleriana* or Fire Hill.

Prunus mume is known as the Japanese Apricot. It is a vigorous bush, normally with pink flowers in March and April, but in gardens is most likely to be seen in one of its good colour forms which will have deeper rose or carmine flowers.

It will be seen that these cover a wide range of forms and types and it is not surprising that they make equally varying demands on the gardener. The Cherry Laurel and Portugal Laurel will grow almost anywhere, in sun or shade, good soil or poor. They can be pruned or clipped in spring or summer and are readily raised from cuttings, either of young growth in summer in a propagating frame or of ripe growth in autumn in an ordinary frame.

The garden varieties of cherry, almond and apricot are often increased by budding in summer on to rootstocks of allied plants, either seedlings of the same species or the stocks used for the fruiting varieties of cherry and apricot. These kinds can also be pruned, but not several times a year like the laurels. Such thinning out or reduction as may be required is best done after flowering. The

Polygonum baldschuanicum

Potentilla fruticosa

Prunus incisa

Rhododendron Ascot Brilliant

Rhododendron
Lady Chamberlain

Rhododendron augustinii

Rhododendron fulvum

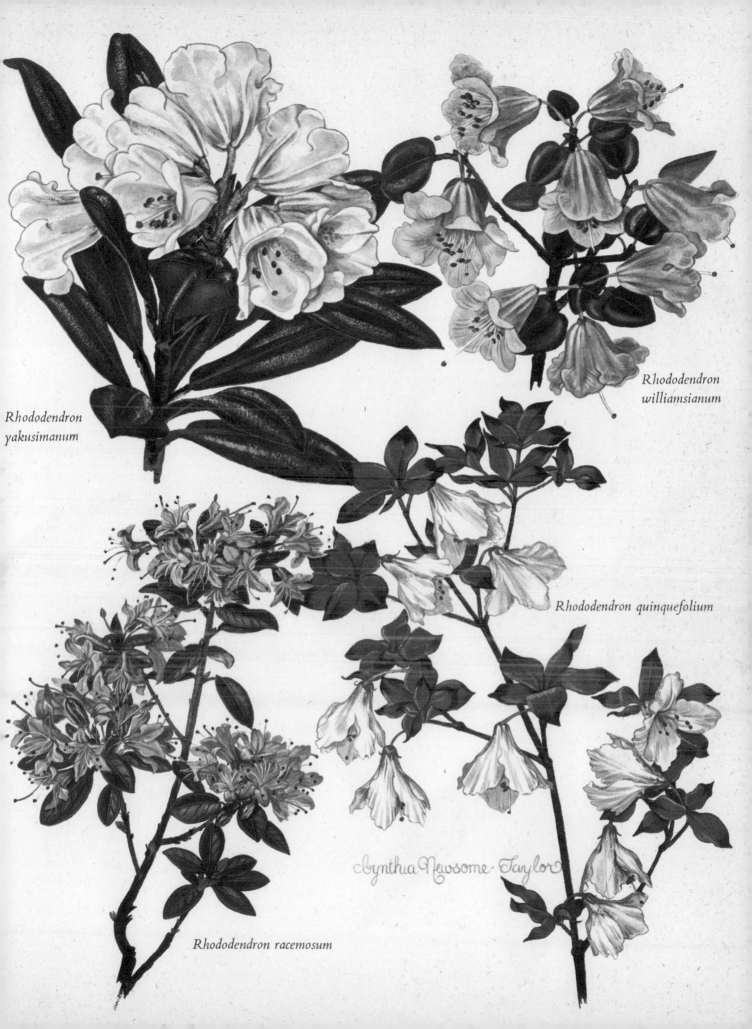

*Rhododendron
yakusimanum*

*Rhododendron
williamsianum*

Rhododendron quinquefolium

Rhododendron racemosum

Cynthia Newsome-Taylor

Prunus
laurocerasus

Rhododendron
williamsianum

Rhododendron
fulvum

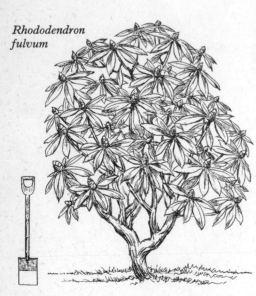

almonds and apricots need sun and warmth and good well-drained soils. The cherries are far less fussy and more easily satisfied and will usually grow in any reasonable soil and sunny position.

PYRACANTHA (Firethorn) Valuable evergreen shrubs grown primarily for their abundant crops of highly coloured berries in autumn, but also for their white flowers in June. All will make big freely branched bushes in the open, but they are frequently planted against walls when they require some pruning to keep them to an acceptable shape.

The most popular variety is *Pyracantha coccinea lalandii* which has quite large orange-red berries. *P. atalantioides*, also known as *P. gibbsii*, has smaller berries but they are produced with such freedom that individual size makes little difference to the display. They are a deeper red than those of *P. coccinea lalandii* and are not so subject to attack by birds. There is a yellow-berried variety, named *aurea*. The Firethorn usually known in gardens as *P. rogersiana* is really a small-leaved form of *P. crenulata* and an excellent plant with scarlet berries. Another form of *P. crenulata*, sometimes called *P. crenulata flava* and sometimes *P. rogersiana fructu luteo*, has orange-yellow berries. Waterer's Orange is close to this, having been raised from seed of *P. rogersiana*.

The Firethorns are all easy to grow in almost any soil. They will thrive in sun or shade and are excellent for clothing north-facing walls. When grown on walls they should be pruned immediately after flowering, badly placed growths which cannot be trained or accommodated being cut out but, so far as possible, without removing the trusses of berries which will then be forming.

Propagation is by seed sown in a greenhouse or frame in spring, or by cuttings of firm young growth in a propagating frame or under mist in June, July or August.

RHODODENDRON This vast genus contains sufficient good ornamental shrubs to furnish large gardens with little assistance from other families. However, a drawback of a garden that relies too heavily on rhododendrons is that it will have a concentration of interest in April and May, tailing off very rapidly after mid-June. The genus includes, in addition to the shrubs universally known as rhododendrons, all those commonly referred to in gardens as azaleas. These latter contain both evergreen and deciduous groups, but the garden rhododendrons are all evergreen. Because of the important differences in character between those groups, I shall deal with them separately, referring to them respectively as rhododendrons and azaleas.

The rhododendrons have an enormous range of habits and styles. There are completely prostrate kinds, such as crimson-flowered *R. repens*; small bushes 1 to 3 feet in height, such as *R. hanceanum nanum*, yellow, and *R. impeditum*, pale purple; bushes of medium size, such as *R. yakusimanum* and the familiar 'hardy hybrid' rhododendrons such as Britannia, Ascot Brilliant, Cynthia and Pink Pearl, in time reaching a height and spread of 10 to 18 feet; and tree-like species such as *R. arboreum*, red, pink or white, and *R. falconeri*, soft yellow blotched with purple.

There is an equal variation in flower shapes and sizes. Some, such as *R. racemosum*, have little flowers less than an inch across, whereas the giant species may have flowers individually 3 inches across, carried in big trusses nearly a foot across. There are nearly flat flowers, as in *R. augustinii* and *R. quinquefolium*; funnel-shaped flowers, as in *R. loderi*; bell-shaped flowers, as in *R. williamsianum*; tubular flowers, as in *R. Lady Chamberlain*, and between the multitudinous species and innumerable hybrids almost every colour is represented. Some of the big-leaved varieties, and those, such as *R. fulvum*, with leaves thickly covered with brown felt beneath, are worth growing simply for their foliage.

Azaleas cover a rather smaller range of sizes and styles, and their colour range does not extend to the purples and blues but is particularly rich in yellows, oranges and coppery-reds. The evergreen kinds, of which the Kurume hybrids are typical, have small leaves and flowers and make fairly low but wide-spreading bushes, usually no more than 3 feet high but anything up to 9 feet in diameter as they age. They flower in April, May and June.

The deciduous azaleas are also usually represented in gardens by hybrids which pass under various group names, such as Mollis, Ghent and Knap Hill, according to the size and character of their flowers or their place of origin. They make fine bushes, 4 to 8 feet high and as much through, and their flowers are usually immensely showy. The commonest species, *R. luteum*, has deep yellow, richly fragrant flowers and the leaves turn crimson before they fall.

It is impossible here to give any representative selection as whole catalogues and books are devoted to rhododendrons and azaleas. Anyone intending to purchase should first visit a nursery or garden in which rhododendrons are grown. There are splendid collections in the Royal Horticultural Society's gardens at Wisley, and in the Savill Gardens in Windsor Great Park. In the North a good collection is being made in the Northern Horticultural Society's gardens at Harlow Car, near Harrogate, and there are a great many public parks and private gardens open to the public which make a special feature of rhododendrons and azaleas.

All dislike lime and thrive best in soils containing a fair amount of peat or leafmould, but they can also be grown in many other types of soil provided they are not alkaline. The purplish-mauve *R. ponticum* has established itself as a wild plant in many parts of Britain, spreading by seedlings which grow quite rapidly into fine evergreen bushes. The common yellow azalea, which has deliciously fragrant flowers, also propagates itself freely by seed, though it has not spread to anything like the extent of *R. ponticum*.

In general rhododendrons and azaleas appreciate some shade, but the hardy hybrid rhododendrons will grow quite well, though rather more slowly, in full sun, and the same is true of the hybrid races of deciduous azaleas.

No rhododendrons or azaleas require regular pruning but all benefit from dead-heading, *i.e.*, the removal of the flower trusses when they fade. The object of this is to prevent seed formation and so allow the plant to concentrate its strength on growth and the production of flower buds for the following year.

Some rhododendrons are so tender that they can only be grown in Britain in greenhouses. These are outside the scope of this book, but there are others, such as *R. macabeanum*, yellow, and *R. griersonianum*, scarlet, which can be grown outside in the milder counties but not in cold gardens. These semi-tender kinds are most likely to prove successful if planted in thin woodland, preferably woodland containing some evergreen conifers which will give protection in late winter and early spring before the deciduous trees come into leaf.

All rhododendrons and azaleas benefit from annual mulches of peat or leafmould, which may be applied at any convenient time of year but are usually put on in spring while the soil is still moist after the winter rain.

All rhododendrons can be raised from seed but the hybrids will not breed entirely true from seed, though the variations produced may be very pleasing. Seed is sown on the surface of sandy peat in February or March and germinated in a frame or greenhouse, the seedlings being pricked off into boxes and later lined out in nursery rows to grow on to garden size, which may take several years. Some rhododendrons and azaleas can be increased by cuttings of firm young growth taken in June or July and rooted under mist, preferably with soil warming. Nurserymen increase many of the named varieties by grafting, usually on to seedlings of *R. ponticum*. This grafting is done in spring in a greenhouse and later the plants are hardened off and planted out.

RIBES (Currant, Gooseberry) The currants and gooseberries of the fruit garden are derived from species of *Ribes*, but there are also ornamental species grown primarily for their flowers. The most popular of these is *Ribes sanguineum*, a quick-growing deciduous bush with pink or rose-red flowers in March and April. It will reach a height of 8 to 10 feet and a spread of up to 12 feet, but can be kept smaller by quite hard pruning immediately after flowering. There are varieties with brighter or larger flowers, notably Pulborough Scarlet which is a rich magenta-red.

Rhododendron hanceanum nanum

Rhododendron (Ghent Azalea)

Rhododendron Lady Chamberlain

Rhododendron
(Kurume Azalea)

Rhododendron (*Azalea mollis*)
Christopher Wren

Rhododendron luteum

Rhododendron (Ghent azalea) garden form

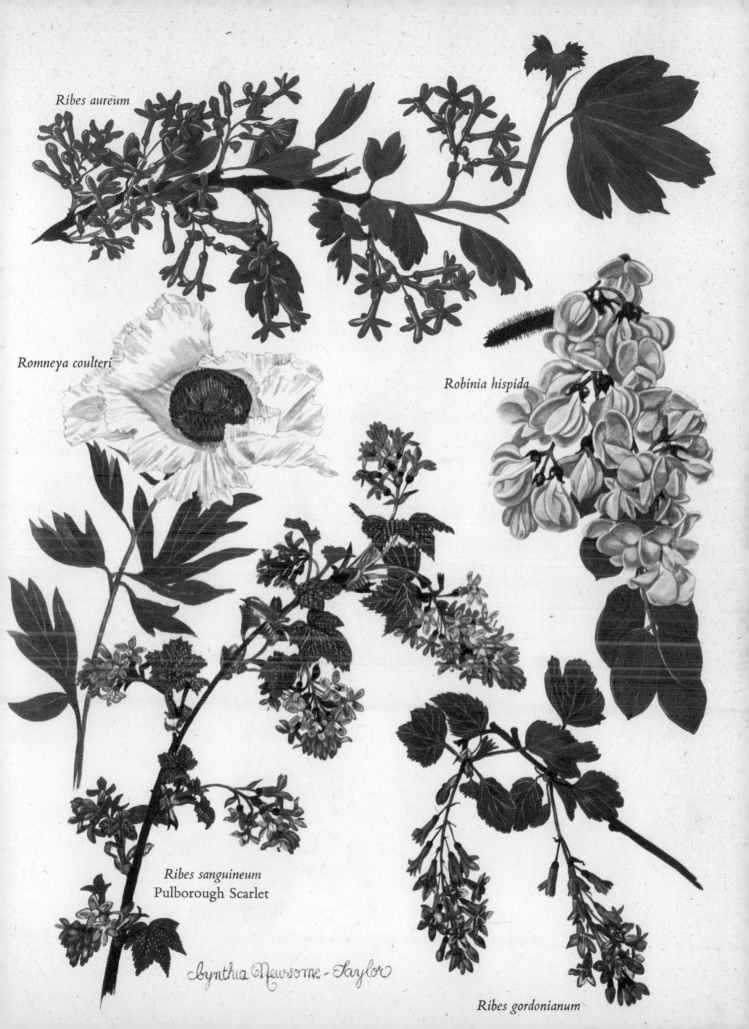

Ribes aureum

Romneya coulteri

Robinia hispida

Ribes sanguineum
Pulborough Scarlet

Cynthia Newsome-Taylor

Ribes gordonianum

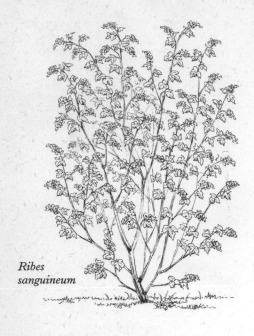

Ribes
sanguineum

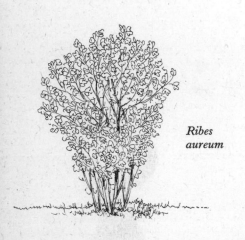

Ribes
aureum

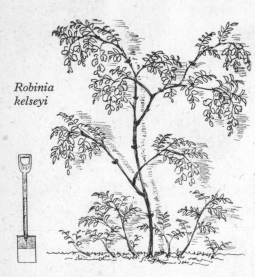

Robinia
kelseyi

Ribes aureum, the Golden Currant, is less vigorous, not exceeding 6 feet in height and about as much through, and it has bright yellow scented flowers in April, followed by black fruits. *R. gordonianum* is a hybrid between *R. sanguineum* and *R. odoratum*, the latter a species very similar to, and much confused with, *R. aureum*. The hybrid is intermediate and has bronze-red and yellow flowers but is not as effective as either of its parents. *R. laurifolium* is an evergreen 4 to 5 feet high and through, with large laurel-like leaves and greenish-white flowers in February.

All will grow in any reasonable soil and sunny or partially shady position. They can be increased by cuttings of firm young growth in summer in a propagating frame or under mist, or the deciduous kinds by cuttings of fully ripe growth in autumn in a sheltered place outdoors.

ROBINIA (Locust, False Acacia) Most species of *Robinia* are trees, but there are shrubby kinds as well, two of the most ornamental being *Robinia hispida*, known as the Rose Acacia, and *R. kelseyi*. Both are deciduous and have rose-pink flowers in June, but *R. hispida* is about 6 feet tall and spreads by suckers whereas *R. kelseyi* is 9 to 10 feet tall and of loose open habit. They delight in well-drained soils and warm sunny places, and should not be planted in very exposed places because of the rather brittle nature of their branches. They can be increased by seed sown in a warm greenhouse in spring, and *R. hispida* can also be increased by suckers dug out with roots in autumn or early spring. Nurserymen often graft on to seedlings of *R. pseudoacacia*.

ROMNEYA (Tree Poppy) The Tree Poppies are only partly shrubby, for though they make stout woody stems during spring and summer, reaching a height of 5 or 6 feet and terminated by large white poppies each with a boss of golden stamens in the centre, most of this growth dies back in winter. There is only one species, *Romneya coulteri*, but this has a variety, named *trichocalyx*, which some gardeners regard as superior, though the differences are very slight. Plants spread by suckers and no limit can be placed to their extent. The flowers appear from July to September and the blue-grey foliage is also decorative. It is best to cut all remaining growth practically to ground level each March or April. Romneya likes a light well-drained soil and warm sunny position. It can be increased by seed sown in a frame or greenhouse in spring, by suckers dug up with roots in early spring, or by root cuttings in late winter or early spring. It is best to grow on seedlings or root cuttings individually in pots, and plant out from these in March or April, as this is a plant that dislikes root disturbance.

ROSA (Rose) All roses are shrubs, but the highly bred garden varieties are usually given such special treatment, both as regards arrangement and management, that they are scarcely thought of as shrubs by gardeners. As they have been dealt with in many books devoted entirely to them, and really do require this special treatment, I shall not include them here.

This leaves all the wild or species roses which truly behave like shrubs and are so considered by gardeners, and also a number of garden varieties which make big bushes and are seen to best advantage in company with shrubs. There are a great many of these and they are a wonderfully diversified lot. Some are grown primarily for their flowers, some for their leaves, their fruits or even for their thorns.

It is convenient to discuss shrub roses in groups according to the species from which they have been derived or to which they seem to be related. Thus *Rosa alba*, a hybrid so ancient that no one knowns for certain its parentage, has given its name to a group of beautiful shrub roses all of which have blue-grey foliage. Nearly all make big bushes, 5 to 7 feet high and as much or more through. Celestial has double shell-pink flowers, Maiden's Blush is flesh-pink and Queen of Denmark a deeper pink which pales as the flowers age. All bloom in June or July.

The Bourbon Roses, known as *R. borboniana*, are also of hybrid origin but their parentage is known as they had their origin at the end of the eighteenth century. They are not quite so tall as the *alba* roses, 4 to 6 feet in height and diameter, and in general they have larger fuller flowers produced over a longer season. Mme Pierre Oger, with big globular pale rose-pink flowers, is one of the most beautiful, and Gipsy Boy, deepest crimson, one of the most richly coloured.

The Cabbage Rose, or *R. centifolia*, is also noted for the size and fullness of its flowers. Varieties of this group make bushes from 4 to 6 feet high and often as much as 7 or 8 feet through. The Old Cabbage Rose with rose-pink flowers belongs here, and so do Tour de Malakoff, a glorious mixture of carmine and purple, and Fantin Latour with large, flat-topped, pale pink flowers. All flower in June.

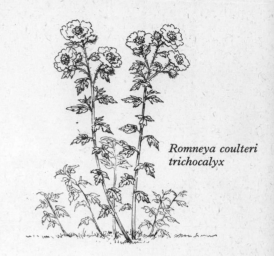

Romneya coulteri trichocalyx

The Moss Rose is really a particular form of Cabbage Rose distinguished by the moss-like growth around the flower stems and calyces. Old Pink Moss, with rose-pink flowers, and William Lobb, a particularly vigorous plant with blue-purple flowers, are favourites.

The China Roses, *R. chinensis*, are usually miniatures. Cécile Brunner is one of the most popular, a bush 3 feet high and through carrying perfectly formed but tiny flesh-pink roses more or less continuously from June to October. Bloomfield Abundance is similar in flower but makes a bigger bush.

The Damask Roses, *R. damascena*, are of very ancient origin. They make fine bushes anything from 4 to 8 feet high and usually a good deal broader than this. York and Lancaster, also known as *damascena versicolor*, with white flowers heavily striped with pink, is one of the most famous, though not the most reliable. St Nicholas is a smaller bush than most, with semi-double rose-pink flowers, and Madame Hardy has well-shaped white flowers. All bloom in June or July.

The French Rose, *R. gallica*, is also of great antiquity though many of the popular varieties are of quite recent origin. Most do not exceed 3 feet in height, but they spread considerably and may be fully twice as broad as they are high. Belle Isis makes a big sprawling bush with flesh-pink flowers, Camaieux is striped rose on a soft pink ground, Rosa Mundi is striped carmine on white, Red Gallica or *gallica officinalis* is semi-double and light crimson, and Belle de Crécy is soft rose, lilac and purple.

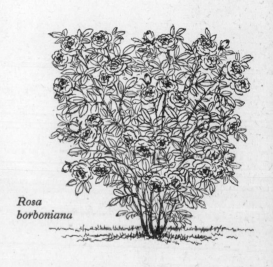

Rosa borboniana

The Musk Rose, *R. moschata*, has produced numerous garden hybrids, though some of the varieties that appear in this class seem to have little claim to Musk Rose parentage. However, all are excellent shrub roses, some very big, reaching a height and spread of 8 or 9 feet, but most 6 or 7 feet high and through. Excellent varieties are Penelope, cream and shell pink; Cornelia, rose-pink; Prosperity, white; Felicia, blush pink; and Magenta, purplish-lilac. They flower from June to September.

The Sweet Briars, *R. rubiginosa*, are noted for the fragrance of their foliage, particularly strong after rain. They make big bushes up to 8 feet high and through. Good varieties are Lady Penzance, coppery-orange, and Anne of Geierstein, deep rose-red. They flower in June and July.

The Rugosa Roses, *R. rugosa*, are very vigorous though they vary considerably in height. Some, such as Blanc Double de Coubert, white, and Rosaraie de l'Haÿ, deep magenta, will reach a height of 7 feet, whereas others, such as Frau Dagmar Hastrup, pale pink, and Snowsprite (Schneezwerg), white, are not above 4 feet, but all will spread in time to a breadth of 7 or 8 feet. Hybrids of *R. rugosa fimbriata*, such as Pink Grootendorst, pink, and F. J. Grootendorst and Grootendorst Supreme, red, have small flowers with fringed petals like a carnation. All flower between May and September but are at their best in June.

Rosa damascena versicolor

The Scots Briars, *R. spinosissima*, have small leaves and make very dense prickly bushes. All spread considerably, sometimes to 10 or 12 feet, and some, such as *altaica* with single creamy-yellow flowers in May, are 7 or 8 feet tall, but most are more compact and only 3 to 4 feet tall. Stanwell Perpetual has larger flowers than most, double and white flushed with pink. William III has small crimson flowers.

In addition to these fairly clearly defined groups there are numerous modern

Rosa rubrifolia

Rosa damascena versicolor

Rosa pomifera duplex

Rosa rugosa Roseraie de l'Haÿ

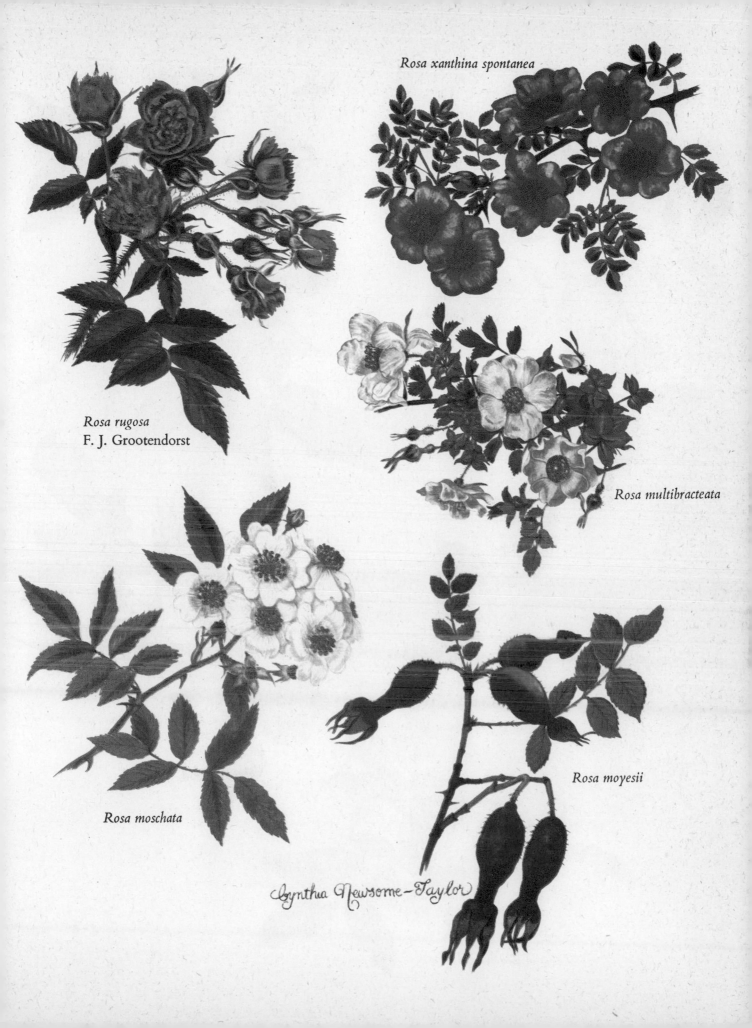

Rosa xanthina spontanea

Rosa rugosa
F. J. Grootendorst

Rosa multibracteata

Rosa moschata

Rosa moyesii

Cynthia Newsome-Taylor

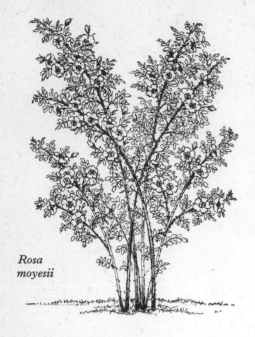

Rosa moyesii

Rosa spinosissima

Rosa rubrifolia

shrub roses which it is difficult to assign to any group. Frühlingsgold and Frühlingsmorgen are of this type, both big bushes with arching branches carrying respectively creamy-yellow and cream and pink flowers. Bonn is rose-red, Elmshorn is carmine, Wilhelm crimson, Nevada creamy-white, and there are many more.

In addition to all these there are the species themselves. *R. moyesii* is a big rather gaunt bush, 8 to 10 feet high and even more through, with velvet-crimson flowers in June followed by large flask-shaped scarlet heps. *R. pomifera* has pink flowers followed by large globose fruits rather like little scarlet apples. A splendid form of this, known as *R. pomifera duplex*, or Wolley-Dod's Rose, has greyish leaves, deep pink semi-double flowers and big scarlet heps.

Rosa nitida is no more than 3 feet high but may spread to 10 or 12 feet. The flowers are carmine, the young shoots are red and the foliage turns crimson before it falls in autumn. *R. rubrifolia* is also grown primarily for its foliage which is blue-grey shot with pink. The small pink flowers are followed by crimson heps. It grows 7 or 8 feet high and about as much through.

Rosa omeiensis pteracantha is grown primarily for its immense thorns, so broad that they join together like translucent bronze-pink wings along the stems. Its flowers are white and come in May and it makes a huge bush, 10 feet high and even more through.

Rosa xanthina spontanea, also known as Canary Bird, also flowers in May, and is a very beautiful shrub with golden-yellow flowers produced in great profusion. It can be 7 feet high and 10 feet through after a few years. *R. multibracteata* is very graceful and distinct, a 6-foot bush of arching stems covered in tiny leaves and small but very numerous deep pink flowers.

All these shrub roses are easily grown in any reasonably well cultivated soil and open situation. They require far less pruning and attention than the hybrid tea roses. Some of the older wood should be removed annually, either immediately after flowering or in autumn or winter. Dead or diseased wood should also be removed and, if bushes grow too large, they can be cut back considerably at any time between October and March.

The species can be raised from seed sown in a frame or outdoors in spring, but hybrids and selected garden forms will not breed true from seed and must either be increased by budding between midsummer and mid-August on any of the stocks normally used for garden roses, or by cuttings. These are of two kinds, summer cuttings of firm young stems (those that have just produced flowers will serve very well) rooted in a propagating frame or under mist, or cuttings of fully ripe growth in October in an ordinary frame or sheltered place outdoors. When these shrub roses are grown on their own roots, *i.e.*, are not budded on to an alien stock, any suckers they produce can be dug out with roots in autumn or winter and will provide an easy means of increase as they will reproduce all the qualities of the parent plants.

ROSMARINUS (Rosemary) The Common Rosemary, *R. officinalis*, has been cultivated for many centuries and is much admired as a handsome evergreen of moderate size, with narrow fragrant leaves and lavender-blue flowers which, in warm sheltered gardens, may commence to open in winter but are at their best in May. Typically it is 4 or 5 feet high and about as much through but there are many varieties differing in habit. Miss Jessup's Upright and *pyramidalis* are both taller and narrower whereas *R. officinalis prostratus* is almost flat and spreading and will actually grow downwards if planted on top of a dry wall or terrace. Corsican Blue, Benenden Blue and Tuscan Blue are all varieties with deeper or brighter blue flowers.

All these, and particularly *prostratus* which is rather more tender than most, like light well-drained soils and warm sunny positions. The erect varieties benefit from some trimming and shortening after flowering as this helps to keep growth dense and prevent the slight straggliness to which Rosemary is prone. All can be easily increased by summer cuttings of firm young growth inserted in a propagating frame or under mist.

RUBUS (Bramble) The blackberry, loganberry and raspberry of the fruit garden are all derived from species of rubus, but there are also ornamental species suitable for the shrub border or wild garden. One of the most beautiful is *Rubus deliciosus*, a big loosely-branched deciduous shrub, 8 to 10 feet high and through, with single white flowers in May. However, it is a difficult shrub to propagate and, for that reason, nearly always hard to buy. This fault is not shared by *R. tridel*, a hybrid between *R. deliciosus* and *R. trilobus* which is similar in dimensions and habit to the former and has even larger and more numerous white flowers in May.

Rubus odoratus make a thicket of growth, 7 or 8 feet high and of indefinite spread, with single light magenta flowers from June to August. *R. ulmifolius bellidiflorus* looks rather like a blackberry in growth and is a big sprawling shrub requiring a good deal of room. Its flowers are very attractive, fully double pink pompons freely produced in July and August.

Rubus illecebrosus is known as the Strawberry-Raspberry because its large red fruits, which follow white flowers, do look remarkably like strawberries. It makes a bush 3 or 4 feet high and as much through.

Rubus phoenicolasius is the Wineberry and makes canes up to 10 feet in length. It is best trained around a pillar or against a wall, where its handsome canes, densely covered with crimson bristles, can be seen to best advantage. The white flowers in June are followed by light red raspberry-like fruits.

Several species have stems that look as if they had been white-washed and are particularly striking in winter when they have lost their leaves. One of the best of these is *R. cockburnianus*, often known as *R. giraldianus*, a loosely branched rather sprawling shrub, 6 or 7 feet high and 8 or 9 feet through, with small purple flowers in June, followed by black fruits.

All these brambles are easily grown in almost any soil and open or partially shaded positions. *R. deliciosus* and *R. tridel* prefer a fully sunny place and *R. odoratus* prefers shade. Most can be pruned quite severely in late summer or autumn but *R. deliciosus* may resent hard pruning.

The species can be raised from seed, but not double-flowered forms or hybrids. All can be increased by cuttings of firm young growth in summer in a propagating frame or under mist, and most can also be layered in summer. Those with long whippy growth like the blackberry will usually respond to tip-layering, *i.e.* the pegging down to the ground of the tips of young stems in June or July. *R. deliciosus* is the most difficult to increase and is best layered but the layers may take many months to form roots.

RUSCUS (Butcher's Broom) The only species grown in Britain, *Ruscus aculeatus*, is a useful evergreen because it will thrive even in dense shade. It grows 2 to 3 feet high and at least as much through and has stiff sharp-pointed 'leaves' that are, in fact, not leaves at all but flattened stems modified to perform the functions of a leaf. This can be seen very clearly when the plant is in flower or fruit, for the small whitish flowers and shining scarlet fruits are borne in the centres of these 'leaves'. There are two sexes and only the female bears the showy fruits and then only if there is a male bush in the vicinity to fertilise its flowers. Butcher's Broom will grow in any reasonable soil and sunny or shady position and can be increased by division in autumn or early spring.

SAMBUCUS (Elder) The Common Elder, *Sambucus nigra*, though a very handsome wild plant, is scarcely worth a place in the garden, but it has several varieties which certainly are. Best of these is *aurea*, with golden-yellow leaves. It makes a big loosely branched bush 10 to 12 feet high and through. Another variety, *laciniata*, has leaves so deeply and finely divided that they look like the fronds of a large fern.

Sambucus canadensis is very much like *S. nigra* in habit but has much bigger heads of white bloom; great plate-like clusters that may measure 10 or 12 inches across. They come a month or so later than those of the Common Elder, in August and September.

All will thrive in almost any soil and in full sun or partial shade. They can

Rosmarinus officinalis

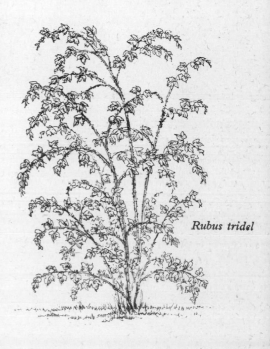

Rubus tridel

Ruscus aculeatus

Rubus tridel

Rosmarinus officinalis

Rubus ulmifolius bellidiflorus

Ruscus aculeatus

Sambucus nigra laciniata

Schizophragma hydrangeoides

Siphonosmanthus delavayi

Santolina virens

Senecio laxifolius

Sarcococca hookeriana digyna

Cynthia Newsome-Taylor

Sambucus nigra laciniata

Santolina chamaecyparissus

Sarcococca hookeriana digyna

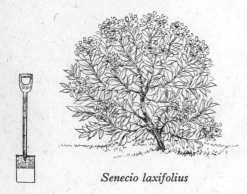

Senecio laxifolius

be cut back quite severely each March or April, treatment which restricts their overall size but increases the individual size of leaves and flower trusses. They are easily increased by cuttings, either of firm young growth in summer in a propagating frame or under mist, or of fully ripe wood in autumn in a sheltered place outdoors.

SANTOLINA (Lavender Cotton) These small evergreen shrubs, with strongly aromatic foliage, are useful for the front of the border. The most popular is *Santolina chamaecyparissus*, which has silvery-grey leaves and yellow flowers in July. It grows about $1\frac{1}{2}$ feet high and 2 to $2\frac{1}{2}$ feet through. *S. virens* resembles it closely except that the leaves are bright green. *S. neapolitana* is a little taller and has more finely divided grey leaves. All like well-drained soils and open sunny places. They benefit from fairly close trimming, which can be done with shears, each spring, as this keeps them neat and dense. They can be increased by cuttings inserted in sandy soil in a frame at practically any time.

SARCOCOCCA Evergreen shrubs which have the merit of flowering in winter and thriving in shady places. *Sarcococca hookeriana digyna* is one of the best as its small pinkish-white flowers are very fragrant. It grows 4 or 5 feet high and may spread considerably by suckers which can easily be dug out and provide a useful means of increasing the plant. *S. humilis* is smaller, around 2 feet, and also has scented white flowers. *S. ruscifolia* is 3 to 4 feet high, has white flowers and broader leaves. All like cool rather moist soils well supplied with humus. They can be increased by suckers or by cuttings of firm young growth in summer in a propagating frame or under mist.

SCHIZOPHRAGMA Vigorous self-clinging deciduous climbers closely resembling the Climbing Hydrangea. One obvious difference is that the sterile flowers, which make the flower trusses conspicuous, consist of one large white or cream bract per cluster instead of several smaller bracts as in the hydrangea. *Schizophragma hydrangeoides* is the most frequently planted, a vigorous plant climbing like an ivy by aerial roots to 20 or 30 feet. The flower clusters measure 8 or 9 inches across. Those of *S. integrifolium* are even bigger, up to 1 foot across. Both like good rich soils, not liable to dry out badly in summer but not waterlogged in winter. They will grow in full sun or partial shade and need no pruning. They can be increased by layering in spring or early summer, or by cuttings of firm young growth in summer in a propagating frame or under mist.

SENECIO This is the genus which has given us such different plants as the groundsel, one of the most troublesome of annual weeds, and the cineraria, one of the showiest of greenhouse annuals. But it has shrubby species as well and, though most of these are too tender to be grown outdoors in Britain, there are hardy or nearly hardy kinds as well. One of the toughest is *Senecio laxifolius*, often wrongly called *S. greyi*, a wide-spreading grey-leaved evergreen shrub producing abundant yellow daisy-flowers around mid-summer. It will grow 3 or 4 feet high and as much as 6 feet through and, though it can be injured by severe frost, it usually comes through the winter safely.

Senecio cineraria, with deeply cut almost white leaves, is usually regarded as a summer bedding plant, but in well-drained soil it is moderately hardy and can be treated as a permanent shrub near the coast and in the milder parts of the country. It will make a handsome bush, 2 feet or thereabouts in height and about 3 feet through. It has yellow flowers in summer but is grown for its foliage.

Senecio rotundifolius has round, thick, shining green leaves and is useful in coastal areas because it will withstand any amount of salt-laden wind. It is said to grow to a height of 30 feet in New Zealand, where it is native, but in this country is commonly seen as a dense dome-shaped bush 3 or 4 feet high and rather more through. It is too tender for inland gardens.

Senecios like light well-drained soils but are not really fussy so long as they do not get waterlogged in winter. They should be grown in a sunny place and can be trimmed to shape each spring. They are easily increased by cuttings of firm young growth in summer in a propagating frame or under mist.

SIPHONOSMANTHUS This is the new name by which gardeners must learn to recognise an old friend, for the deliciously fragrant evergreen formerly known as *Osmanthus delavayi* has become, through botanical reclassification, *Siphonosmanthus delavayi*. It remains a splendid shrub, densely bushy in habit, 9 or 10 feet high and through, with neat shining leaves and innumerable small white flowers in April. It will grow in any reasonably good soil and sunny or partially shady position, and requires no pruning. Propagation is by cuttings of firm young growth in June or July in a propagating frame or under mist.

Siphonosmanthus delavayi

SKIMMIA Evergreen shrubs grown primarily for their scarlet berries, though their flowers also have considerable attraction. The most popular species is *Skimmia japonica*, a rather slow-growing well-branched shrub that will eventually reach a height of 3 feet and spread of 4 or 5 feet. It has little spikes of white fragrant flowers in May and June, followed by shining scarlet berries, but there are two sexes and the berries are only produced by the females, and then only if there is a male bush in the vicinity to fertilise their flowers. There are at least two specially good male forms, one named *fragrans* because it has particularly fragrant flowers, another named *rubella* because the young stems and flower buds are dark red.

Another species, *S. reevesiana*, usually known in gardens as *S. fortunei*, generally produces male and female flowers on the same bush and has passed on this useful characteristic to a hybrid between it and *S. japonica* named *S. foremanii*. This is in many ways the best skimmia to grow as it is easier than *S. reevesiana* and does not require a male bush for pollination like *S. japonica*. It resembles the last named in appearance and habit.

Skimmia japonica and *S. foremanii* will grow in almost any soil but *S. reevesiana* does not like limy or chalky soils. All do best in partial shade. No pruning is required. The species can be raised from seed sown in frame or greenhouse in spring, but seedlings of *S. japonica* may be of either sex. Selected garden forms and hybrids should be increased by cuttings of firm young growth in summer in a propagating frame or under mist.

Skimmia japonica

SOLANUM Two species are grown in the milder parts of the country but are too tender for cold gardens. The hardier of the two is *Solanum crispum*, a sprawling or semi-climbing shrub that can be trained on a wall or over a trellis or outhouse. In favourable places it will reach a height of 20 feet but is usually less. The flowers are purplish-blue and yellow, shaped like those of the potato for which reason it is sometimes called the Chilean Potato Tree, and freely produced from June to September. The other species, *S. jasminoides*, is more slender in growth and produces its white or blue-tinted flowers from July to October. It needs a particularly warm sheltered place. Both species will grow in any reasonably good soil and prefer those that are well-drained in winter. They can be increased by layering in spring or summer, or by cuttings of firm young growth in summer in a propagating frame or under mist.

SORBARIA Splendid deciduous shrubs closely allied to, and resembling, *Spiraea*. *Sorbaria aitchisonii* grows to 9 or 10 feet and may become considerably more through in time by reason of suckers which gradually spread outwards. The small creamy-white flowers are produced in large plume-like sprays in July and August. *S. tomentosa* closely resembles this but *S. arborea* is even stronger in growth and, left to its own devices, may reach a height of 12 or 15 feet. It has a variety with narrower leaves named *glabrata*. All species, however, can be pruned hard each March, treatment which will reduce their height but increase the size of their flower sprays. All have most attractive foliage. They like good soils not liable to dry out in summer, and open or lightly shaded places. They can be increased by digging out rooted suckers in autumn or winter, or by cuttings of firm young growth in a propagating frame or under mist in summer.

SPARTIUM (Spanish Broom) The only species, *Spartium junceum*, is a tall deciduous shrub which carries its yellow fragrant flowers on thin green stems. It makes a rather gaunt bush, 9 or 10 feet high and 6 or 7 feet through, but it is

Solanum jasminoides

Skimmia japonica (flowers)

Solanum jasminoides

Skimmia japonica (fruits)

Spartium junceum

Sorbaria arborea glabrata

Spiraea arguta

Spiraea bumalda Anthony Waterer

Staphylea pinnata

Stachyurus praecox

Stranvaesia davidiana salicifolia

Stephanandra tanakae

Spiraea menziesii triumphans

Cynthia Newsome-Taylor

Spartium junceum

Spiraea veitchii

Spiraea arguta

all the better for trimming each spring which will keep it more compact and at the same time improve the display. It is specially useful for flowering over a long period from early July to late August, and the cut flowers last well in water. Like other brooms, it does not readily make new growth from the hard old wood, so pruning should not go beyond the previous year's growth. It likes light well-drained soils, does well on chalk or limestone and can most readily be increased by seed sown in spring in greenhouse, frame, or even outdoors.

SPIRAEA This big genus of deciduous shrubs contains some delightfully ornamental material for the garden and collectively covers an exceptionally long flowering season. First to flower is *Spiraea thunbergii*, a shrub notable for its mass of thin twiggy branches wreathed in tiny white flowers in March and early April. It grows 4 or 5 feet high and as much, or rather more, through and, as it stands pruning well, can be used to make a small flowering hedge. Right on its heels comes *S. arguta*, a hybrid between it and *S. multiflora*. This is a little larger in all its parts than *S. thunbergii* and continues in bloom until early May, when it is joined by *S. vanhouttei*, another hybrid with *S. cantoniensis* and *S. trilobata* as its parents. *S. vanhouttei* is a very showy shrub, 8 or 9 feet high and as much through, with long arching branches carrying a great many quite large clusters of white flowers. The leaves are blue-green in summer and turn to yellow and crimson before they fall in autumn. *S. cantoniensis* is itself a good garden plant in its double-flowered form, known both as *lanceata* and *flore pleno*. This is 5 or 6 feet high and 7 or 8 feet through, with long arching branches and very numerous fully double pure white flowers in June.

Another very fine double-flowered kind is *S. prunifolia plena*. It will grow 5 or 6 feet high and through and has arching branches bearing, in late April and May, little clusters of white flowers. The green foliage turns to orange and crimson in the autumn.

Spiraea veitchii and *S. canescens* are both June-flowering species making big broad bushes, 10 to 12 feet high and through, with long arching branches bearing along their length little erect stems each terminated by a fine cluster of white flowers.

Very different from all these are *S. salicifolia*, *S. douglasii*, *S. tomentosa* and *S. menziesii* all of which make dense thickets of stems terminated by spike-like clusters of rose-pink flowers. *S. douglasii* is the strongest growing, to 8 feet in height, and can become a nuisance by spreading far and wide by means of suckers. The others are rather less vigorous, 5 to 6 feet high, but still tend to be invasive. The most showy is a form of *S. menziesii* named *triumphans*, which has larger clusters of more richly coloured rose flowers. It will continue to flower from about midsummer to August. So will *S. japonica*, a shrub 5 or 6 feet high and usually rather more through, with flat heads of rosy-red flowers. With another species, named *S. albiflora*, it has produced an excellent hybrid, named *S. bumalda*, which is shorter and more compact in habit, seldom exceeding 3 feet. From this a particularly fine variety has been selected and named Anthony Waterer. Its flat flower heads are deep carmine and many of its leaves are either wholly cream coloured or are heavily splashed with cream.

Spiraea bullata also has flat heads of deep carmine flowers in July and August and is even more dwarf than Anthony Waterer, seldom exceeding 18 inches.

All these spiraeas will grow in any reasonable soil and an open or partially shady situation. The early-flowering kinds, such as *S. thunbergii* and *S. arguta*, benefit from some thinning and shortening as soon as they have flowered. Strong-growing kinds, such as *S. menziesii*, *S. salicifolia* and *S. douglasii*, can be cut back to within a foot or so of ground level each March. Similar treatment applied to *S. japonica* and *S. bumalda* will reduce their height and increase the size of the flower clusters.

All spiraeas can be increased by cuttings, either of firm young growth in summer in a propagating frame or under mist, or of fully ripe growth in autumn outdoors. Those spiraeas that make suckers can also be increased by digging these out with roots in autumn or winter. The very vigorous *S. salicifolia*, *S.*

douglasii and others of this group are all the better for being lifted and divided every few years.

STACHYURUS   There are only two species of stachyurus and they are very similar in appearance. Both *Stachyurus praecox* and *S. chinensis* are deciduous shrubs 7 to 10 feet high with 2- to 3-inch-long trails of yellow flowers in February and March. Like many other winter-flowering shrubs they need a rather sheltered position to protect their flowers from injury, but growth itself is seldom damaged by frost. They like cool soils, well supplied with humus, not waterlogged in winter, yet not liable to dry out severely in summer. No regular pruning is required. Propagation is by cuttings of firm young growth in June or July in a propagating frame or under mist with soil warming.

STAPHYLEA (Bladder Nut)   Deciduous shrubs of vigorous habit which derive their popular name from the inflated bladder-like seed-vessels. The two species commonly grown are *Staphylea colchica*, which carries its creamy-white flowers in more or less erect sprays, and *S. pinnata*, which has drooping sprays of white flowers. There is a hybrid between the two, named *S. elegans hessei*, which has the flower habit of *S. pinnata* but the flowers are tinged with red. All flower in May and early June. They like a reasonably good soil not liable to dry out in summer, and prefer a sunny position. No pruning is required. They can be increased by cuttings of firm young growth in summer in a propagating frame or under mist.

STEPHANANDRA   Deciduous shrubs related to the spiraeas and resembling some species of these. *Stephanandra incisa*, also known as *S. flexuosa*, grows 3 or 4 feet high and 6 or 7 feet through. The leaves are so deeply lobed as to be almost fern-like and in autumn they turn yellow before they fall. The small greenish-white flowers are produced in feathery sprays in June. *S. tanakae*, the only other species cultivated, has less divided, and therefore less decorative, leaves but the autumn colouring is richer and so is the reddish-brown of the stems, which in winter can be quite a feature. It grows 5 to 6 feet high and 7 to 9 feet through.

These are moisture-loving plants which revel in good rich soils beside a pool or stream, though they can also be planted well away from water so long as the soil does not dry out badly in summer. They will grow in full sun but *S. incisa* prefers a shady place. They can be increased by division in autumn or winter or by root cuttings in winter or early spring.

STRANVAESIA   Under favourable conditions all the stranvaesias can attain tree-like proportions, but in British gardens *Stranvaesia davidiana* is more commonly seen as a large shrub, 12 to 15 feet high and as much through, with leathery evergreen leaves and sprays of white hawthorn-like flowers in June, followed by scarlet berries. There is a variety of this, named *salicifolia*, with narrower leaves and another, named *undulata*, in which the edges of the leaves are wavy, and this does not grow anything like so tall, being only about 5 feet high and through. Typically this has similar scarlet berries but there is a form of it, named *fructu-luteo*, with yellow berries. All like well-drained soil and sheltered positions. They require no pruning. They can be increased by seeds sown in a warm greenhouse in spring, or by cuttings of firm young growth in summer in a propagating frame or under mist with soil warming.

SYMPHORICARPOS   Only two species of symphoricarpos are commonly grown in gardens, both for their berries. One, *Symphoricarpos albus*, better known to most gardeners as *S. racemosus*, is called Snowberry because these globose fruits are pure white. The other, *S. orbiculatus*, is known as Coralberry or Indian Currant because its much smaller fruits are purplish-red or pink. There is a variety of this with golden-variegated leaves. The best variety of *S. albus* is named *laevigatus*. It is more vigorous and has finer berries. Both *S. orbiculatus* and *S. albus laevigatus* make densely twiggy bushes, 6 to 7 feet high and spreading indefinitely by suckers. Their flowers, dull white in *S. orbiculatus*, pink in *S.*

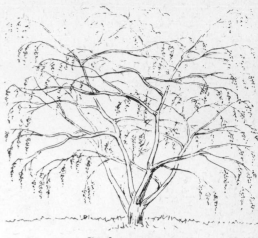

Stachyurus praecox,
in blossom

Symphoricarpos albus
laevigatus

Stephanandra
tanakae

Syringa yunnanensis

Symphoricarpos albus laevigatus

Syringa microphylla

Syringa vulgaris Souvenir de Louis Späth

Cynthia Newsome-Taylor

Trachelospermum jasminoides

Viburnum bodnantense

Tricuspidaria lanceolata

Vaccinium corymbosum

Tamarix pentandra

Ulex europaeus plenus

Syringa
Bellicent

Syringa microphylla

*Tamarix
tetrandra*

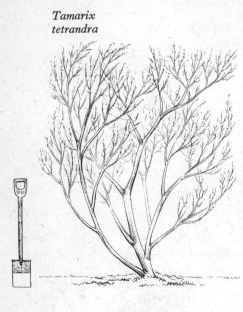

albus, are too small to make much display. They thrive in any reasonable soil and open or shady position and if desired can be trimmed occasionally in spring and summer to make a screen or hedge. They can be increased by division in autumn or winter, by cuttings in a frame in autumn, or by seed in a frame in spring, but the variegated variety will not come true from seed.

SYRINGA (Lilac) The fragrant Common Lilac of gardens is *Syringa vulgaris* and it has been cultivated for so long that a great many varieties have been developed. These differ in the size, colour and character of their flowers and may be divided into single-flowered and doubled-flowered groups. Typical of the former are Charles X, purple; Souvenir de Louis Späth, reddish-purple; Marechal Foch, rose paling to mauve; Clarke's Giant, soft blue; Maud Notcutt, white; and Primrose, primrose-yellow. Good double varieties are Charles Joly, purple; Katherine Havemeyer, soft mauve; Michael Buchner, rosy-lilac; Paul Thirion, rosy-red; Madame Antoine Buchner, soft mauve; and Madame Lemoine, white. All flower in May and make large bushes, a good 15 feet in height when fully grown and nearly as much through.

In addition there are some very attractive wild species, though not many of them have the sweet fragrance of *S. vulgaris*. However, fragrance is a characteristic of *S. persica*, the Persian Lilac, a bush to 6 feet high with small sprays of lavender flowers in May. It is also found in the Rouen Lilac, *S. chinensis*, a hybrid between *S. vulgaris* and *S. persica*, nearly as tall and vigorous as the former, with lilac-coloured flowers in May.

Syringa josikaea, known as the Hungarian Lilac, is another big shrub with loose sprays of deep lilac flowers in early June. *S. reflexa* and *S. villosa* resemble it but are more beautiful, the former with partly drooping sprays of lilac-pink flowers, the latter with very large loose sprays of lilac-rose flowers. These two have produced a race of hybrids, collectively known as *S. prestoniae*, with all the qualities of elegance and vigour of their parents and a wider colour range. Some of the best forms have been named and these include Bellicent, lilac-rose; Isabella, mallow purple, and Hiawatha, reddish-purple. Another hybrid is between *S. josikaea* and *S. villosa* and this is named *S. henryi*. It has pale purple flowers. *S. yunnanensis* also belongs to this group of large shrubs with narrowly tubular flowers, in this species lilac-pink.

Syringa microphylla is often wrongly called *S. palibiniana*. It is quite a small bush, 4 to 6 feet high and as much through, with little rounded leaves and small but abundant sprays of deep lilac flowers in May.

All lilacs will grow in any reasonably good soil and open position. Pruning is not essential but if the faded flower trusses can be removed it helps the bushes to flower more freely the following year. The species can be readily increased by seed sown in greenhouse or frame in spring, but hybrids and selected garden varieties will not breed true from seed. If they are on their own roots, *i.e.* are not grafted on to a stock, they can often be increased by digging out rooted suckers in autumn or winter. Nurserymen usually increase the garden forms of *S. vulgaris* by grafting or budding on to seedlings of that species, in which case suckers will be of the seedling type. Lilacs can also be layered in spring or summer, and cuttings of young or half-ripe growth can be rooted in summer in a propagating frame or under mist.

TAMARIX (Tamarisk) These graceful shrubs, with plumy sprays of tiny pink flowers, have a special utility because they will withstand salt-laden winds and so can be used in seaside gardens. For this the best species is *Tamarix gallica*, which grow 8 or 10 feet high and 5 or 6 feet through and flowers in July and August. It is not as decorative as *T. pentandra*, the most beautiful species, with blue-grey leaves and much larger sprays of rosy-pink flowers. This will reach a height of 10 or 12 feet and spread of 8 to 10 feet, but can be kept considerably smaller by pruning. It flowers in July and August. *T. tetrandra*, which is similar in habit, flowers in May and June.

All like light well-drained soils and open sunny places. *T. gallica* and *T. pentandra* can be pruned quite severely each March. The pruning of *T. tetrandra* is best left until it has flowered, when old branches can be cut out and younger ones shortened. All can be increased by cuttings of firm young growth in June or July in a propagating frame or under mist, or by cuttings of fully ripe growth in October in sandy soil outdoors.

TRACHELOSPERMUM *Trachelospermum jasminoides* is a very fragrant but rather tender evergreen twiner which can be grown on a sunny wall or similar sheltered position. The leaves are dark green and glossy, the flowers white, rather like those of a summer jasmine, and produced in July and August. It will reach a height of 10 or 15 feet. There is a variety, named *variegatum*, with cream-variegated leaves, and another, named *wilsonii*, with leaves of variable shape, some quite narrow, some broader and some turning crimson in autumn. All like reasonably good light soils, preferably with the addition of some peat or leafmould, and warm sunny positions. No regular pruning is required. They can be increased by cuttings of firm young growth in July or August in a propagating frame or under mist with soil warming.

*Tricuspidaria
lanceolata*

TRICUSPIDARIA Only one species is at all commonly grown in British gardens but it suffers from having two quite different names. Usually it is known as *Tricuspidaria lanceolata* but sometimes as *Crinodendron hookerianum*. This is almost certainly wrong, that name belonging to another, white-flowered species seldom grown in Britain, but probably the correct name for our plant is *Crinodendron patagua*, by which it would certainly not be recognised by British gardeners. It is an exceedingly distinctive and beautiful evergreen, 10 feet or more in height and 5 to 7 feet through, with hanging crimson lantern-shaped flowers in May and June. It is not very hardy and in many parts of the country needs the protection of a west- or south-facing wall, but in mild places and near the coast can be planted fully in the open. It likes lime-free peaty soils and a moist atmosphere, conditions similar to those appreciated by some of the more tender rhododendrons. No regular pruning is required. It can be increased by cuttings of firm young growth in June or July in a propagating frame or under mist with soil warming.

*Ulex europaeus
plenus*

ULEX (Gorse) The common gorse, *Ulex europaeus*, in its normal single-flowered form, though an extremely handsome shrub, is too common a wild plant to be worth planting in gardens, but it has a double-flowered variety which certainly is worthy of consideration. This is named *plenus* and it gives a tremendous display of golden-yellow bloom in April and May. It makes a broad intensely spiny bush 4 to 5 feet high and as much as 6 or 7 feet through. Two other species, both of supposedly dwarf habit, are sometimes grown. One, *U. nanus*, will remain at a height of about 2 feet in poor sandy soil but may reach more than twice that height in rich soil. It is much like the common gorse in appearance but flowers in early autumn. The other, *U. gallii humilis*, may be no more than 6 inches high, though 3 to 4 feet through, and flowers in August.

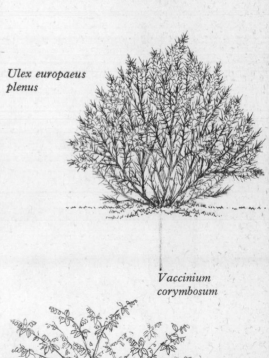

*Vaccinium
corymbosum*

All like poor sandy or stony soils and sunny positions. If desired they can be pruned in May, or after flowering, to prevent them becoming straggly. They are increased by cuttings of firm young growth in summer in a propagating frame or under mist.

VACCINIUM (Blueberry, Cranberry) This is a big genus of shrubs several of which are useful ornamental plants for shady places, though none is in the first rank for beauty. *Vaccinium corymbosum* is the Blueberry, grown, amongst other things, for its richly flavoured blue-black berries. It is deciduous and its leaves turn scarlet before they fall in autumn. It will grow 4 to 6 feet high, occasionally considerably more, and is 6 to 8 feet through when full grown.

Vaccinium myrsinites is sometimes known as the Evergreen Blueberry because it retains its leaves, is about 2 feet high, occasionally a good deal more, and has small white flowers in April and May, followed by black fruits.

Vaccinium myrtillus is the Bilberry or Whortleberry of British moorlands and mountains, a low spreading shrub with pale pink flowers in May, followed by

Viburnum opulus sterile

Viburnum tinus

Viburnum burkwoodii

Weigela florida variegata

Viburnum opulus compactum

Wisteria sinensis

Vitis coignetiae

Zenobia pulverulenta

Cynthia Newsome-Taylor

Yucca flaccida Ivory

Viburnum bodnantense

Viburnum davidii, in fruit

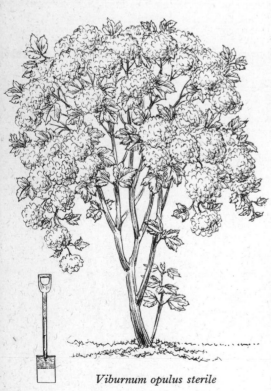

Viburnum opulus sterile

blue-black berries. Its North American counterpart, very similar in habit and size, is *V. caespitosum*. The Cranberry, with red fruits, another native shrub of almost prostrate habit, is *V. macrocarpum* and will throw out 3-foot creeping stems with pink flowers in spring, also followed by red fruits. There are many more. All are shrubs for cool rather moist peaty soils and shady or sunny positions. They can be increased by seed sown in greenhouse or frame in spring, or by cuttings of firm young growth in sandy peat in a propagating frame or under mist in summer.

VIBURNUM This important genus contains a wealth of beautiful and varied ornamental shrubs. *Viburnum tinus* is one of the most familiar, popularly known as Laurustinus, a big bushy evergreen with clusters of white flowers, tinged with pink in the bud in some forms, which will sometimes begin to open in December and continue throughout the winter until April. It will grow 7 to 10 feet tall and through. There is a variety, named *variegatum*, with cream-variegated leaves.

Another fine evergreen is *V. rhytidophyllum*, a shrub that will quickly reach a height of 10 or 12 feet and spread of 8 feet, with big leaves, dark green and wrinkled above and covered with grey felt beneath, broad flattish heads of dull white flowers in May, followed by showy scarlet berries.

Viburnum davidii is a low-growing evergreen, 2 to 3 feet high and up to 5 feet in diameter, with dark green shining leaves, small white flowers and turquoise-blue berries which are more likely to be produced if several bushes are planted.

Viburnum carlesii is deciduous and makes a loosely branched bush 4 to 5 feet high and a little more through. Its flowers, pink in bud, white when open, are produced in small but abundant clusters in April and May. They are intensely fragrant. *V. utile*, an evergreen of similar habit and size with white flowers in May, is chiefly famous as the parent, with *V. carlesii*, of an excellent hybrid named *V. burkwoodii*. This is deciduous, 6 to 8 feet high and rather more through, with large clusters of fragrant white flowers in April. Even larger flower heads are produced by *V. carlcephalum*, a hybrid between *V. carlesii* and *V. macrocephalum*, the last a big partially evergreen bush with hydrangea-like heads of white flowers. One further hybrid of *V. carlesii* which merits attention is named *V. juddii* and has *V. bitchiuense* as its other parent. It resembles *V. carlesii* closely but often flowers more freely.

Viburnum fragrans and *V. grandiflorum* both flower in winter, commencing in November and continuing until March or April. Both make erect deciduous bushes, 9 or 10 feet high and 7 or 8 feet through. The small clusters of flowers are pinkish-white in *V. fragrans*, deeper pink in *V. grandiflorum*. There is an excellent hybrid between these two, named *V. bodnantense*, which closely resembles *V. grandiflorum* but is particularly hardy and free-flowering. Also in this group of deciduous winter-flowering kinds is *V. foetens*, with pure white flowers. All are very fragrant.

Then there are the early-summer-flowering kinds, of which the British Guelder Rose, *V. opulus*, is a notable example. This handsome bush is too freely distributed in the wild to be worth introducing to gardens in its common form but it has some excellent varieties, including the Snowball Bush, *V. opulus sterile*, in which the white flowers, instead of being in flat heads, are arranged in the form of a ball. It is a deciduous bush, 10 or 12 feet high and through, flowering in late May and early June. There is also a useful variety, named *compactum*, no more than 6 feet high, with the normal type of flower heads followed by shining currant-red fruits. Another variety, named *xanthocarpum*, has yellow fruits.

The same contrast between flat and ball-like flower heads, but on a smaller scale, is seen in *V. tomentosum* and its variety *plicatum*. These, too, are deciduous, 9 or 10 feet high and rather more through, and they flower in May. There are several improved forms of the flat-headed type, of which *mariesii*, with flower-heads of superior size, arranged along the length of horizontally held branches, is one of the best.

Viburnum betulifolium is grown primarily for its immense crops of small currant-red fruits. The white flowers in flat heads come in June and July.

All viburnums grow readily in most soils and reasonably open, sunny positions, though *V. foetens* is said to prefer a partially shaded place. Most need little or no pruning, but the display of the horizontally branched varieties of *V. tomentosum* can be improved if the central stem is cut out when it has reached a height of about 4 or 5 feet. This encourages the development of the broad spreading habit which displays the flowers to perfection, particularly if the bushes are planted where they can be viewed from above.

Those species which produce berries freely can be raised from seed sown in frame or greenhouse in spring. The evergreen kinds are best raised from cuttings of firm young growth in summer in a propagating frame or under glass. The deciduous kinds can also be raised from cuttings in the same way, or by cuttings of fully ripe growth in October in a frame or sheltered place outdoors. *V. fragrans* often layers itself freely and these can be dug up in autumn or winter.

VITIS (Vine) Most of the ornamental vines which gardeners have been accustomed to call, and often still do call, *Vitis* have been removed to the genus *Parthenocissus* where they are described in this book. But the grape vine itself remains *Vitis vinifera* and has several useful ornamental varieties, while another very decorative species is the large-leaved *V. coignetiae*. This will easily reach a height of 20 or 30 feet, is an admirable climber to run into an old tree or over a large outbuilding, and has leaves up to 12 inches across which turn yellow, orange, scarlet and crimson before they fall in autumn. Of the grape vine varieties two of the most ornamental are Brandt, the leaves of which turn to pink, crimson and orange before they fall, and *purpurea*, with leaves that are red or purple throughout the summer.

These vines like good loamy soils and sunny positions. When grown for ornament, they need not be pruned, but if good fruit is required from Brandt it is best to cut back many of the side growths to within an inch or so of the main rods each winter. All can be increased by cuttings of ripe growth in October or November in a frame.

WEIGELA These deciduous shrubs have been known as *Diervilla*, and may still be found under that name in gardens and nurseries. They are amongst the most showy and easily grown of early-summer-flowering shrubs. The commonest species is *Weigela florida*, a loosely-branched shrub, 6 to 8 feet high and through, with rose-pink flowers all along the stems in late May and June. It has a variety, named *variegata*, with cream variegated leaves and pale pink flowers.

Weigela middendorffiana is very distinct, only 3 or 4 feet high, with sulphur-yellow flowers spotted with orange, but it needs a sheltered place as it is none too hardy. *W. japonica* will reach 7 or 8 feet and has flowers that are pale rose at first but deepen to carmine as they open. *W. floribunda* is similar in size, has arching branches and deep crimson flowers.

However, it is not these species but the garden varieties raised from them, and particularly from *W. florida*, *W. floribunda* and *W. japonica*, that are most important as decorative shrubs. There are a considerable number of these, varying in flower size and also in colour, from white to crimson. Among the best are Abel Carriére, soft rose; Eva Rathke, crimson; Newport Red, deep carmine; and Styriaca, rose.

All will grow in any reasonably good soil and open position. They benefit from pruning immediately after flowering, when the flowering stems can be cut back as far as young shoots or stems that have not yet flowered. They can be readily increased by cuttings, either of firm young growth in summer in a propagating frame or under mist, or of fully ripe growth in October or November in a frame or sheltered place outdoors.

WISTERIA The very familiarity of the wisteria is apt to obscure the fact that this is not just one climbing plant but a genus of several quite distinct species each with varieties of its own. The commonest in cultivation is *Wisteria sinensis*, the Chinese Wisteria, a very vigorous climber easily capable of reaching a height of 20 or 30 feet, with densely packed flower trails 9 or 10 inches long.

Viburnum tomentosum mariesii

Vitis coignetiae

Weigela florida variegata

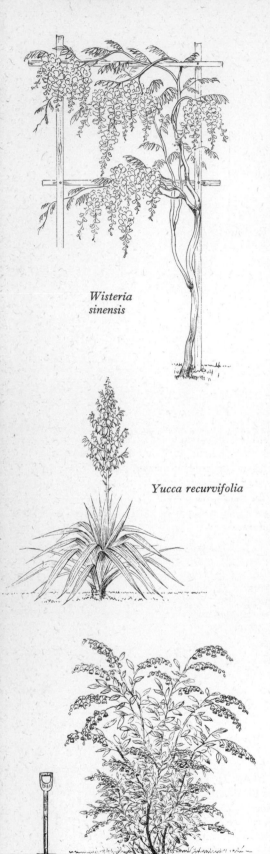

*Wisteria
sinensis*

Yucca recurvifolia

Zenobia pulverulenta

The colour can be variable, in the poorest forms a rather greyish-mauve, in the best quite a lively blue-mauve. There is a variety with white flowers, named *alba*.

Wisteria floribunda is the Japanese Wisteria, not quite such a vigorous climber as *W. sinensis* but even more variable not only in flower colour but also in the length of its flower trails. Some poor forms may have flower trails little longer than those of the Chinese Wisteria, but in the best forms, of which that known as *macrobotrys* or *multijuga* is typical, the flower trails may be 2 to 2½ feet long. Usually they are light violet-blue, but there is a white variety, named *alba*, a flesh pink variety, named *carnea*, a warmer pink variety, named *rosea*, a deep pink variety, named *rubra*, and a double-flowered violet-blue variety named *violaceo-plena*.

Wisteria venusta is known as the Silky Wisteria because of the silky down on its leaves. The flower trails are quite short, not above 6 inches, but the individual flowers are large and white. Like the other species it flowers in May and June.

All wisterias are deciduous. They are not fussy about soil but prefer those that are reasonably rich. They like sun and do well on south- or west-facing walls or trained over large pergolas in the open. It is possible to form them into shrubs, or even into standards with a head of branches on a long bare trunk, by systematic pruning each July, when all young growths not actually required to extend the plant can be cut back to 5 or 6 inches. If this treatment can be applied to mature plants that have been allowed to climb they will produce more and better flowers, but to prune a really large wisteria can be a considerable task.

Plants are best increased by layering in spring or early summer. Seedlings are apt to vary too much in quality.

YUCCA These evergreens of highly exotic appearance make great rosettes of stiff sword-shaped leaves from which arise in summer stout spikes of creamy-white cupped flowers. They are much hardier than they appear and several kinds can be grown successfully out of doors in most parts of the country. Hardiest of all is *Yucca filamentosa*, which will make basal rosettes 2 or 3 feet high and through and produce from these in August 5-foot stems of flowers. There is a handsome variety, named *variegata*, in which the normally blue-green leaves are striped longitudinally with lighter green and yellow. *Y. flaccida* is much like *Y. filamentosa* in appearance and hardiness but is less stiff in habit. Some authorities consider it to be a variety of *Y. filamentosa*. It has a particularly good form named Ivory.

Yucca gloriosa, sometimes known as Adam's Needle though this name is also applied to *Y. filamentosa*, is the giant of the hardier kinds. In very sheltered places it can reach a height of 8 feet, making a distinct trunk carrying several large rosettes of stiff leaves. The flowers appear in late summer and are carried in sprays 4 feet long and up to 1 foot wide. *Y. recurvifolia* resembles it in many ways but is not so tall and the leaves are not straight but bend outwards and downwards. A big old specimen with several rosettes may measure 8 or 9 feet across. It flowers in July and August.

Yuccas like light well-drained soils and warm sunny places. They do well by the seaside and often, also, in town gardens. They require no pruning but it is desirable to cut out the flower-stems when the flowers have faded. They can sometimes be increased by offsets detached with roots in spring, and also by root cuttings in winter or spring in a warm greenhouse or frame.

ZENOBIA There is only one species in this genus, *Zenobia pulverulenta* (also known as *Z. speciosa*) and this is not often seen, though it is a beautiful and distinctive evergreen. It grows to 6 feet high and through, has blue-grey leaves and loose terminal spikes or sprays of white bell-shaped flowers in June and July. It belongs to the heather family and needs a lime-free soil, either a loamy or peaty soil for preference though it will also grow in sandy soils. It can be planted in a sunny or partially shaded place and requires no pruning. It can be raised from seed sown in sandy peat in a frame or greenhouse in spring but is usually increased by cuttings of firm young growth in July or August in a propagating frame or under mist with soil warming.

INDEX

to popular and catalogue names